Kaleidoscope

of

Polyamory

How ready are you for an open relationship?

MINT RABBIT

Table of Contents

Introduction

You might be surprised to find out that monogamy is not the dominant form of relationships on our planet today. In Western society, there are many who prefer to be in love relationships with several people at the same time.

According to cultural experts, polygamy is allowed in 83% of the world's societies. [1] Does the traditional, formal concept of a family we are all familiar with really reflect the essence of what actually happens in reality?

Just imagine. Some people have couples next door, colleagues from work - decent husbands and wives, boys and girls living in pairs. Some of them, in opinion polls and questionnaires, talk about a slightly different kind of relationship. Other characters enter the scene — and they are close to each other no less than people in regular couples.

"This is not my husband's friend. This is his lover. And mine. Our. There are three of us. We are happy."

"Oooh, Hi! How was your week?" Two couples meet and go to spend the evening in a restaurant with a glass or two of wine. The usual friendly gathering. Pleasant evening. We admire them. Their warmth of communication. The restaurant closes and everyone leaves, to continue their evening together. The atmosphere changes from warm and friendly to hot and sexy. There, behind the closed doors of the house, the whole company is happy. The next day, things resume as usual.

"Friends, we love you. See you! Bye, Bye!"

And here is another couple, it seems that they were happy, but the routine, this routine of family life, it turns prose into delicious poetry.

"Maybe we'll try and take a chance?"

"Well, I don't mind ..."

Oooh ... they'd better be bored ... Pain, jealousy, misunderstanding, feelings fading, and the couple is parting. End of the line: divorce.

Surely some person was visited by a very intense sensation or thought from somewhere deep within, from the very depths of their subconscious - this feeling of loneliness, or craving for eternal love, the dream of living together forever with their special someone, or that uncomfortable feeling that the society is not built in the way that would suit perfectly to the cravings of their soul. Social customs do not completely correspond to one's desires, aspirations and lifestyle. And what a blessing it is when you find like-minded people and soul mates who are in tune with you! After uncovering these soulmates, society, relatives, colleagues, and neighbors — despite still having their opinions, — will not be able to influence the choice of that person´s path.

With this book, you will have the opportunity to get familiar with the amazing new kind of relationships where, as in a kaleidoscope, you will see a variety of fascinating figures and shapes and colors. By handling it carefully and skillfully, you can get an infinite supply of colorful patterns to grant you lots of aesthetic pleasure. Or with a single awkward movement you can destroy the mosaic of colors and patterns and remain disappointed, if not broken.

You might be interested to know that this subject is as much about yourself as other people. Let all the thoughts and facts and stories described here become for you a mirror, an instrument for better self-understanding. Let no one force you to do anything that you do not accept. And let all that you want, happen to you!

So, have a nice time exploring the Polyamory Kaleidoscope!!!

Chapter 1
Types of Relationships: Single, Monogamy, Polygamy, Varieties of Marriages

The modern world is replete with a variety of options.

What was impossible to imagine 50 years ago is accessible to everyone today, to everyone who has at least a little inner freedom and an open mind. The world has changed and continues to change every day at tremendous speed. The timeless values are not as timeless as many have thought, and the forbidden fruit is not that forbidden.

Literature and cinema have installed certain patterns of behavior in our minds and cultures. And we follow them, sometimes without thinking whether they correspond to our inner self. After all, every one of us is unique, and at the same time, woven from universal particles of energy, thoughts, and desires.

We are used to the fact that love has always played out according to the same scenario, right? A man falls in love with a woman, they get married, they have children, and until the end of their lives, they maintain a harmonious, monogamous relationship.

But today we see can more and more people who do not want to simply or automatically follow the scripts of their parents or grandparents.

The first type of relationship that we will talk about in this chapter is having no relationships at all, staying single.

Single

In front of me there is this CD with a popular song. Not an album where the atmosphere or mood is created by a number of songs carefully chosen, but one single song! The music is so beautiful that it does not need the added support of other compositions.

By itself. One. But not alone. Self-sufficient.

Human beings come into this world alone and leave it alone. And some, quite consciously, continue to remain in the same self-sufficient and independent state for the whole of their lives.

Previously, age reflected your position within local hierarchy: the older you get, the higher is your status. Today, those boundaries and definitions are really blurred. Some of us, approaching the age of 30, still do not know who we will become "when we grow up." Mobility, the rejection of routine, the desire to postpone starting a family, the pursuit of a creative profession or hobbies aren't yet considered or planned. For those older, this may seem like infantilism or immaturity.

Millennials are called young adults — "YOUNG adults.

25–44 years — young adult age,

44–60 years — middle age,

60–75 years — old adult age, or advanced age,

75-90 years — elderly age [2]

Over 90 years — long-livers. This is the best definition you can come up with. The younger generation is not in a hurry to give birth to children and has a rather demanding approach to relationships: their relationships must be comfortable and should not suppress their personality, or should not exist at all. They want to do everything they can to avoid in their personal lives any negative experiences causing depression or career failures. Investing in relationships means wasting time, and not everyone is ready for this today.

> Irene, 27:
>
> It makes me crazy when they tell me: "you are already 27, it's time to think about getting married and starting a family." You need to have a child before you turn 30! Seriously, I just don't understand. Am I really an adult? The world is so huge, there are so many opportunities in it — I want to re-read and review a bunch of everything, I like to travel or just sit at home in silence, stay awake all night and go to meet the dawn, paint the picture by numbers for 20 hours in a row or sleep until dinner. Yes, I want to try anything and everything! Just leave me alone. I'm fine!"

As a result of dramatic change in values, single people appeared. These are people who want to be single, who do not seek to create romantic relationships, but rather want to focus on other things and areas important and interesting to them. They focus on work, traveling and creativity while putting aside emotional and sexual connections. There is also another meaning of being a single person — one who is simply not ready to devote him- or herself to a long-term monogamous relationship or enter into an official marriage. They see things in a way that a full spiritual and physical connection with a partner should be something unpredictable and spontaneous. While they are not necessarily looking for a partner, they are open to it when it happens.

These "New Singles" support the idea that marriage is no longer a prerequisite for happiness. They build their lives outside the old system of strictly defined values. At the same time, it is difficult to call them selfish: they easily converge with other people, make new friends and may even have a long-term boyfriend or girlfriend. However, they do not tend to get hung up on the partner. They derive energy primarily from self-development and creativity.

These "Loners" are typically very strong emotionally. They know that you can rely on yourself, and that everyone has their own battle to fight. They try to find a reasonable explanation for each difficult situation. Loners never give up and become stronger with every failure or mistake.

Nick, 38 years old:

"For 10 years now, I am in a state of "self-sufficiency." Some time ago, I went through a rather difficult break with my girlfriend. Later, a flurry of blows of fate fell upon me. My sister and her husband died in a car accident, and I was the only one who could take care of their two children. I focused only on that. I had to cope with all the responsibilities for their education. And now they are already independent young people, and I'm used to being a loner. I like it. During this time, I managed to channel my pain and desire to be with someone into creativity and self-education. I became a different person. It seems to me that I can handle everything. Am I likely to create a couple with someone? Maybe. But I'm not sure if I need it..."

Liza, 45 years old:

As far as I can remember, I have always been in love. And, of course, I was married. It was fun. But everything comes to an end sometime. My husband and I broke up 8 years ago. Finally, I don't have to rush home, I have a lot of friends, interesting things to do, meetings, my work... And I used to think that I must be paired with a man, because a single woman is indecent ... and should, should, should ... all that horrified me! So, I said to myself, "Ahaha... That's enough! I am all by myself, and at the same time I'm never alone. I like being single!"

There are a lot of such people among us. They are able to balance between the state of loneliness and freedom. Today everyone is free to choose their own way.

What are the prospects for sexual life of singles of humankind in the future? Toys, sexual robots, Virtual Reality (VR)-porn — all this allows you to reach a high-quality orgasm alone, without unnecessary efforts and risks coming from another person.

The popularity of such leisure is growing. The number of VR-porn requests on PornHub, for example, had increased by 440% only in 2016. According to the data for 2019, VR-porn steadily takes third place in the search for a sexual partner.

Sex robots are becoming more personalized, learning to speak and joke; and finally, manufacturers are developing male models for women. They promise that in the near future, robots will become even more human-like — for example, they will begin to sweat and release grease. Having such toys, why would you need sex with other people?

Scientists have even come up with a name for such a sexual "orientation" of the future — "digisexuality." A person with this orientation will have sex mainly or exclusively with objects, NOT with another human being. On the one hand, there is nothing wrong with that. On the other hand, critics believe that "digisexuality" dehumanizes sex — and this can lead to a new wave of violence against people, especially against women. [3]

The next object of our research is a person who prefers to be in partnership with only one partner, that is, in a monogamous relationship.

Monogamy

Monogamy (from Greek words, μόνος "single" + γάμος "marriage") is a form of marriage and family in which a person has only one partner during his or her life, or at any given time.

The fact is that, historically, monogamy has not always been related to love. Monogamy began to flourish when our ancestors began to lead a sedentary lifestyle. Men relied on women's loyalty to know exactly whose children they had and who would inherit the herds and fields.

Thanks to monogamy, it was also easier for fathers to share valuable property — for example, land, — among their children.

This is mainly for women. But what about the men?

Everyone knows that in Islamic culture, it is perfectly normal for one man to have several wives. If you look at the historical and economic features of life in the eastern countries, you are more likely to give a positive assessment of this phenomenon (if you do not take into account, of course, a certain percentage that does not favor the lives of women in such marriages).

In any case, be it East or West, throughout history, men have had permission to have several wives, or infidelity/adultery has a minimal amount of consequences for men. All this was supported by a number of biological and evolutionary theories. They justified the need for men to wander, and therefore be in violation of monogamy. And, finally, this double standard was developed: woman is congenially monogamous, and man is a natural polygamist.

In the idealistic Victorian society of the 19th century, the concept of "monogamy" was replaced by the concept of "romantic love." "The idea that a sexual partner should be the only one came up not so long ago," says law professor Hadar Aviram of Hastings College of Law in San Francisco, California, USA.

Poleyev wrote: "This is a very important and complex phenomenon. A big, real romantic love usually happens to a normal person one, perhaps two times, or usually a maximum of three times in a lifetime. It cannot happen more often, and for the following reason: although the feeling of romantic love is very joyful, bright and exciting, it is as well exhausting, both psychologically and physiologically! The feeling of romantic love is not based on emotions at all, as it might seem, and is not about not passion (although emotions and passion are present undoubtedly!). The true base of romantic love is so-called double mistake of thinking. First of all, it is idealization, when we perceive an otherwise ordinary person as unusually smart, attractive beyond example, and extraordinary in any other respect as well. Very often, idealization occurs despite the fact that we know the real virtues of a person. The second mistake of thinking is the idea of uniqueness. When it seems that only with this person you will be able to find your happiness." [4]

Erich Maria Remarque: "Life is too long for love alone..." [5], [6]

Nevertheless, monogamy in the studies of sociologists and psychologists is more a cultural product than a biological one.

On the one hand, steady long-term relationships surely provide stability and promote order in society. On the other hand, they endanger the very survival of the human species. Indeed, if one of the spouses dies or becomes unable to participate in sexual relations, the chances of continuing the human race in nature with monogamy are reduced to zero.

Therefore, behind the visible formality of the organization of society in the form of traditional family cells, lies the unbridled energy of the thirst for life and the continuation of oneself in the maximum number of offspring possible.

What is the actual percentage of people who choose polygamy? It's hard to say for sure.

The definition of infidelity is constantly expanding. Some persons who are in monogamous relationships consider sexting, watching porn, and secret use of dating apps as forms of infidelity. Since there is no common understanding of what the definition of infidelity includes, the percentage of non-monogamy varies from 26% to 70%.

In addition, we are walking contradictions. Approximately 95% of us will say that it is bad when a partner lies about love affair. And about the same share of people plan to do the same if they have the opportunity.

Very often people monogamous in their beliefs find themselves in a conflict between their values and beliefs. Often these are people who have been faithful for decades. But one day he or she crosses the line and risks losing everything, by becoming "UNfaithful."

For many, there is yearning or a lack of something in their relationships. There is a thirst for emotional connection, novelty, freedom, independence, intensity. The desire to regain lost parts of yourself. Attempts to regain vitality in the face of loss. Without self-awareness, rather innocently, they find themselves on the path to new sensations that seem to be available only in new relationships.

So, what is monogamy in the modern world?

Some time ago it was considered monogamy when you married one person, for life. Today it means one person at a time. In the old days, we got married and only after taking marriage vows we had sex for the first time. Now we get married and stop having sex with others.

Having a romantic ideal, we are looking for it in one person. We want our partner to be the best friend, lover, attorney, emotional friend, to match our intellectual level, and so much more. We want them to be everything we think we need and want in a mate. Choosing a person according to these parameters, we let them know that he or she is the only one. But can everyone accept another person, not only with their wonderful qualities, but also with the whole depth of the dark side of their personality? And this dark side, of course, is present in everyone.

We live in an era when we feel that we have the right to satisfy all our needs. We live under the new motto: "I deserve to be happy." In the past, we got divorced because we were unhappy. And today it often happens because we could have been happier. Earlier, divorce was associated with shame; today, staying married when you could leave for a different choice is a new shame.

But what if passion has an expiration date? What if there are things that even a good marriage is not able to provide?

The modern world has provided to a woman the right to vote, the opportunity to earn money, to own property, and decide what to do with her body and life.

Thus, an incredible amount of directions and forms of relationships and marriage are now open for women.

The early XX century writer Vladimir Gilyarovsky in his work "Moscow and Muscovites" wrote about a proverb that was popular in his days: "Every merchant has a husband — by law, an officer — for the senses, and a coachman — for pleasure."[7] This proverb is also relevant today. A woman cannot combine all of her needs in one man, so she can assume that she needs several. Psychologists call this psychological non-integrity.

In modern times, men found themselves in an equal choice with those who were their property yesterday. They had either to embrace these new rules, or to choose alternative forms of relationships, including gender.

Society is gradually becoming more prepared to accept any form of relationship and marriage. Any of these forms become available and depend more on peoples' own preferences rather than on prescriptions.
So, we smoothly move on to the following relationship model:

Polygamy

Polygamy (from the Greek. Πολύς - "numerous" and γάμος - "marriage") is a form of marriage in which a spouse has more than one marriage partners of another sex.

Polygamy is something ordinary and recognized in world society. According to the ethnographic atlas of George Murdoch, of the 1231 societies described in the 1960-1980s, 186 were monogamous and 1041 polygamous. As Joseph Giant, author of *Polygamous Families in Modern Society*, wrote, a third of the world's population are polygamous societies. "This is more common than most people think," explains Jessica Wood of the University of Guelph (Canada). "We are at that stage in the history of society in which we expect too much from our partners. We want sexual satisfaction as well as emotional and financial support. An attempt to fulfill all these requirements puts pressure on relationships." [8]

In her study, Jessica Wood and her colleagues compared the level of happiness and satisfaction among non-monogamous lovers and those who prefer traditional relationships. To 1achieve this end, more than 300 people were invited to take part in the study; 140 of participants were in open relationships, 200 more were in monogamous ones. Participants had answered a number of questions regarding their satisfaction with their current relationship(s). For adherents of free love, the questions concerned their main partners, i.e., non-monogamous unions. [9]

After analyzing the answers of the participants, and comparing them, the scientists concluded that, on average, people who are in monogamous and non-monogamous unions are equally satisfied with their relationship. It turned out that one of the main factors of satisfaction with relationships is not their type, but the nature of sexual motivation. According to them, if in a relationship, you are satisfied psychologically and sexually, then in general you will be happier with a partner. And it does not depend on the type to which your relationship belongs.

Let's take a look at the wide variety of marriage forms known today. There are so many of them, and this diversity proves once again that relationships between people and the form of these relationships are very subtle, delicate and complicated issue that just cannot be judged using the single set of criteria that will always fit perfectly.

Varieties of marriage

White (spiritual) marriage (not to be confused with spiritual as related to church and faith) is a marriage in which spouses deliberately refuse sex and live like a brother and sister, believing that physical attraction can destroy spiritual relationships. It was popular among European nobles in the 18th and 19th centuries. Today, white marriage is often carried out in countries where many seek to emigrate. In this way, people manage to obtain a residence permit or citizenship. True, most countries in Europe and the USA reserve the right to invalidate this form of marriage and send migrants back to their homeland.

Lavender marriage is a marriage between two people of different sexes, in which one or both partners are homosexual, pansexual or bisexual. It is conducted with the aim of "covering up" one's true sexual orientation, in order to avoid condemnation of relatives or society, the creation of a "traditional family" or with the aim of moving up the career ladder and acquiring benefits.

Interfaith marriage is a marriage between representatives of different faiths. Some sociologists associate interfaith marriage with a weakening of religious values, but they do not give an assessment of this phenomenon. Statistics say that interfaith marriages are very common. Twenty years ago, the number of children who were born into such unions exceeded a billion people. [10]

An **organized (or arranged) marriage** is a marriage in which spouses are matched for each other by other people (family members, parents or a professional matchmaker). Psychologists call this type of marriage one of the causes of possible psychological disorders, along with a marriage due to an accidental pregnancy or a marriage which was provoked by a desire to leave the parental home. However, serious cultural differences should be considered, because most psychological studies are conducted with subjects from Western countries.

An **original (creative) marriage** is a marriage concluded between a person and an inanimate (relatively inanimate from the ethics' point of view) subject (doll, robot, gadget, etc.). While humanity perceives this type of marriage with a significant amount of irony, David Levy, author of a book on the evolution of the relationship between robots and humans, predicts that it will be possible to enter into a serious relationship with the machine by 2050. Adrian Cheok, a professor of computer science at City University of London, adds that people will start living with robots much earlier than 2050. [11]

An **open marriage** is a marriage in which the spouses agree that each of them may have extramarital sex and this is not considered infidelity, despite the monogamous nature of the marriage. At the same time, spouses are emotionally attached to each other and perceive "outsiders" only as sexual partners. This type of relationship is one of the most recent. This term first appeared in 1972: the O'Neill couple described it in their book *"Open Marriage: A New Lifestyle for Couples."* True, the phenomenon itself cannot be called new. In the upper classes of Europe, official marriages in fact were open. [12]

Polyamory is the practice of having romantic relationships with several people at the same time. It does not have a direct connection to marriage, it is primarily about love (amor - lat. "love") relationships. "Most people think that polyamory is a sex community. But actually, it's not true..." — said family psychologist Maria Trakova in her interview to Snob web magazine. "This is a community where everyone should be very good at communicating, understanding their needs, setting boundaries and naming desires. And it seems to me that it's sometimes even more difficult than being in a traditional relationship." [10]

Polyandry is a rare type of **polygamy** in which a woman is in several marriages with different men. This exotic type of union is practiced by some peoples in Tibet, but earlier polyandry was much more common. Anthropologists from the University of Missouri have calculated that at least 53 tribes and nations have practiced such relationships. Polyandry is found both in the High North among the Eskimos and in some parts of India.

Polygyny is a type of marriage in which a man has several wives. The best-known name for polygyny is **polygamy**. Interestingly, the majority of polygamy is strongly associated with the world of the East, where a man would not mind "having three wives." This is actually a fallacy. Historically, polygyny has been characteristic of 80% of the world's cultural communities, not only in China and Ancient Greece, but also among the indigenous peoples of America and Africa. [13]

Parental marriage is a marriage concluded between two people (quite possibly, of different orientations) in order to produce and raise children. It lasts until their children reach a certain age. Often this marriage is forced, first of all, for financial reasons, but also because of domestic difficulties.

Starting (trial) marriage is a childless marriage, which consists of a couple (usually young people) in order to test the format of legalized relations. In the future, it either decays or goes to a full form. In essence, this is what is called a "civil marriage".

 A **friendly marriage** is a marriage concluded by a couple as a mutual guarantee of stability and "unity"; in the exact wording "for joint socialization and the implementation of various tasks together." This form of marriage is neither about love, nor about children, nor about passion. [10]

Chapter 2
Forms of Open Sexual Relations: Threesomes, Swinging

There was a Paradise in the Garden of Eden until the moment when temptation made its way into the souls of people. All of us, the descendants of Adam and Eve, carry this within us. We succumb to temptations. Modern culture masterly pushes us into the space of many pleasures. As soon as a person rises from bare survival — basic demands for food, warmth, safety — new spaces of desire opens before them. Take a look around and you will see that the world provides many temptations. These are not only things. We are interested in something more, something that cannot be valued with money. We want more. And more. AND MORE.

What does the story say? Even the biblical patriarch Abraham actually offered his wife Sarah to the Egyptian pharaoh, and then conceived a child with his legal concubine Hagar. His grandson Jacob quite officially had two wives, Rachel and Leah. Catherine the Great, who was in connection with Potemkin, wound up young favorites with his approval. The fatal beauty Lilya Brik lived for many years as a family with her husband Osip and the poet Vladimir Mayakovsky. Psychologist Sigmund Freud entered into an ambiguous relationship with Minna, the unmarried sister of his wife. And this list can be continued for a long time.

There are no conventions and boundaries for the nature of sex. All that you need for sex there is relaxation, freedom and dedication. Normal and natural sex is a game. A game by the rules that you set to yourself. It doesn't matter how others do it and how supposedly it should be.

Many people mix (and are confused about) different concepts of love and sex. Sex is not love and love is not sex. But aren't these things compatible?

I say that they are indeed compatible. These things can be combined or shared. Public attitudes prevent us from doing this naturally. People, following generally accepted rules, try to mix love and sex. The result is an awkward hybrid. In fact, everything is very simple if you could forget about the rules and standards.

But many people are embarrassed or afraid when these instincts wake up within them. They consider it unnatural or sinful. On the one hand, there is a generally accepted framework of decency, which is not always convenient to violate. On the other hand, it is impossible to get satisfaction from sex while staying within this framework. In fear of the awakening of their animal instincts, people begin to enwrap sex with established rituals. This causes some kind of enslavement.

But you can personally determine the rules that are best suited for yourself, and you are not obliged to follow the rules set and promoted by strangers. If you are open and make it clear to your partner what you want to receive, the whole Universe will open back to you! And you may even find that your partner has plenty of hidden desires, too.

To get satisfaction from sexual relations, you need to feel free, liberated.

In 1957, in America, the magazine "Mr." published a sensational story about the exchange of wives during sex. [14] This article was the first sign in the whole series, which talked about new opportunities to revitalize sexual relations in marriage. Later, despite the numerous attacks of moralists, the so called **"swingers"** movement gained recognition, not only in

America, but also in other developed countries (Germany took first place).

How does a "swinging" happen?

To implement the plan, the couple is looking for partners. The safest way is through special clubs. The game goes according to certain rules. It has a tacit code of conduct. It is based on the voluntary desire of partners. Sometimes matching pairs are found on the Internet. However, there is a big risk of running into perverts.

Anna, 26

> Once a polyamorous friend came to us and stayed for two weeks. All this time, in the apartment there was a feeling that threesome sex is imminent. Everyone knew that sex would happen, but no one was in a hurry and everyone were engaged in other activities like sipping rum on a cozy balcony, listening to music, meeting friends, working and going for walks.
>
> This went on for about ten days.
>
> This feeling we had was not deceitful. On Friday night, I returned home drunk and happy. It is a known fact: alcohol adds decisiveness where it is lacking. "Hello, how are you?" someone said, then one thing led to another, and suddenly here I am lying between two guys, one of whom is my beloved man, and the second is a recently acquired friend.
>
> The secret to threesome sex is foreplay. You will get closer to each other, get to know each

other, embarrassment goes away, and sweetness comes in its place — viscous, like honey, and juicy, like the flesh of a peach.

In the process, I set up an experiment. I closed my eyes and tried to guess who was playing with me now: a guy or a friend. First I guessed rather quickly, and then I delved into my feelings, and the boundaries of personalities started to blur. My man becomes my friend, and my friend becomes my beloved man. That is, they two become one. Penetration into me was from both my friend and my partner — but, damn it, I was sure that I had sex with one man. This is the indescribable feeling that extols sex to the rank of mystical practices.

A miracle happened to me — pleasant, mysterious, and unforgettable. I did a blow job to my beloved, and our friend was behind me. While I gently dissolved in my beloved man, a friend entered inside me with all his strength. My partner looked at me and admired.

What did I feel then!? I felt that my partner was everywhere around me. He made love to me from behind, he looked into my eyes, he whispered things into my ear, he was silent; it was him who played the music; that was a night that never ends; a laugh that spills out; and juicy, juicy tenderness in me. There was no one else but him.

Needless to say, I failed to experience any remorse. On the contrary, we have lived through sexual experiences from the category of those that bring couples together and make relationships stronger.

I realized that love could take different images and forms, but the essence does not change from changing names. Threesome sex is such a springboard that scares you at first, and then raises you to breathtaking heights. And yet, this is such a springboard that substitutes the bandwagon, if there is lack of confidence in your couple.

The next morning, we went to the summer terrace of a cafe nearby to have breakfast and drink champagne. It was September, the wind was warm, and the conversations were laid-back. We talked about nothing and smiled sweetly. The aftertaste of sex was in the air.

Having swinging sex can take different forms, depending on desires of the participants:

1. **Easy swinging** — in this case, couples exchange partners only during the prelude, another option for light (soft) swinging is the participation of the third person.

2. **Closed swinging** — after exchanging partners, couples have sex outside of each other's visibility

3. **Open swinging** — exchanging swingers engage in sexual relations in front of each other. Family swingers are not just a new round of the sexual revolution, it is a way to maintain a fading relationship in a safe way.

However, both partners must be mature enough, open-minded and loving. With all manifestations of jealousy and lies, swinging can become a trap that will destroy the marriage. Therefore, each partner in the couple must decide for themselves whether he or she is ready to move to a new step in sexual relations.

Julia, 31 years old:

> When we celebrated the 5th anniversary of our life together, we decided that we needed to somehow diversify our sex life. And our choice fell on a threesome.
>
> So that no one was offended, we decided to first try sex with a third girl, and then with a man. To admit, for the last option I had to persuade my husband for a long time. As it turned out, quite a lot of people are in search of such a relationship.
>
> We had meetings with the "candidates" until we found those we liked. The date was agreed, and when the agreed time had come, we rented a hotel room, ordered dinner with wine and seafood. We started talking and drinking in a restaurant, then moved to our room. Frankly, there was a lot of alcohol. To be blunt, we all liquored up to the point of being drunk.
>
> ..Sex itself turned out, frankly, nothing to shout about. I am not a bisexual, and it

annoyed me greatly that my man caresses another woman.

But I knew that in a week another man would caress me, so I did not give a move of jealousy.

All week after the first attempt at threesome, my husband and I avoided each other so as not to discuss this. A week later, everything repeated, only my husband was already nervous. From a technical point of view, I liked this option much more.

For another week we were silent, trying to stay at work and not discuss our experiment.

Personally, it all disgusted me. And, yes, it seemed to me that we had changed each other. As it turned out, he also thought that. As a result, sexual relations between us faded, we attracted each other no longer, and thoughts of infidelity had led to frequent fights.

After 4 months, we filed for divorce. It was our threesome that caused our break-up. Alas.

Paula, 29 years old

I had a lover and best friend. With my lover, I was hoping that everything would turn into a lasting relationship. And my friend was such a whiner, she loved to be pitied by everyone. And they loved her and pitied her. I also felt sorry for her and loved her.

Therefore, when she began to cry to me that she had no sex for a long time, I invited her to be the third with us, with my lover. Yes, out of pity.

But as a result, the third was me. Literally the third weird. They just forgot about me, although everything happened in my apartment, on my bed.

I did not bother them, went out to smoke, and took a walk. When I returned, they drank coffee in my kitchen and chatted merrily. Giggled, parted. As a result, they started to date, and for some reason started to tell everyone nasty things about me. I guess, this was my friend´s idea, out of jealousy.

By the way, they lived together for four years, but then they broke up.

Leon, 34

It all happened a few years ago with a good friend of mine and her fiancé. They wanted to experiment, but I did not belong to their closest circle. It was a very pleasant experience: that guy and I, without saying a word, decided to give the girl maximum pleasure. I know that after the wedding they had similar adventures.

Since one of the main conditions for swinging is full confidence, a new type of sexual relationship allows swingers not only to strengthen the marriage, but also to add some "zest" to it. After all, it was the thing that was starting to get lacked by couples after several years of living together. Usually, a more active participant begins to look for diversity outside of the couple.

Some Statistics

About 4 to 5 percent of all adults are currently in open or polyamorous relationships;

About 20 percent tried open or poly relationships at some point;

About 17 percent of adults aged 18-44 had sex with someone else with the consent of their partner, compared with 9 percent among adults aged 45-54;

About 28 percent of adults say that it's not natural for a person to be faithful to just one person;

About 29 percent of young people under the age of 30 find open relationships morally acceptable — compared with only 6 percent of adults over 65. [15]

What to avoid in swinging relations

• Do not invite your friend to have threesome sex. You risk losing friendship, and sex can turn into a continuous awkward moment. The ideal third is a friend who lives in another country, and you see him/her no more than twice a year. A casual acquaintance is not a very reliable option, you know too little about him.

• Do not imagine threesome as « *l'amour de trois»* *(French).* This is more of a sexual adventure than romance. It is necessary to immediately make clear to the third that "this is just about sex, nothing personal."

• Do not forget that the third is a supporting role. First of all, you give your affection to your beloved and show how good it is for you to be together with him/her. The third partner is more like a sexual toy that moves and talks and creates an atmosphere.

•Do not be shy. Don't feel ashamed of neither your own desires, nor for the desires / proposals of your partner / partners. Sex is an act where the best you can do is to toss away from your heart and your mind all stereotypes and opinions of other people.

• Do not forget to use condoms or other methods of personal protection. You must be protected on both sides! After each act, a new contraceptive is needed, therefore it is better to immediately open the pack and place it within arm's reach.

• Do not be surprised that the guys could caress each other. After all, his is threesome sex, not the sex of two guys and one lady, all unique and stuff.

• Do not be afraid that threesomes will ruin your relationship. On the contrary, this experience can be a good springboard, an experience that will either bring you both to heavenly new experience or ruin everything for good.

So, before you go looking, ask yourself again - why do you want his? Often, in this way, couples try to solve some long-standing internal problems. However, this is a dead end - relations will only worsen. If this is the desire to avenge or punish - you need to seek help from a family psychologist. When the question "either the third in bed, or we part" is posed with an edge, it is better to disperse right away - anyway the relationship will end there.

Well, if you think that you are ready to experiment, mature enough and confident in yourself and your partner to survive a new experience and get out of it enriched rather than devastated, then this is your story.

Chapter 3
What is Monogamy and Polygamy?

To have sex or to make love?

After all, this is not the same thing! It is one thing to meet and spend time together, sometimes for pleasure, and another thing is to love, live, share responsibilities, help each other, trust, forgive and cherish something more than just the chemistry that arose between you.

We are used to the fact that by default we give it all to a loved one. As a rule, to one. But what if there are two of them? And you cannot divide your heart between them.

In the film "Professor Marston and the Wonder Women" there is a dialogue between the professor and his wife about the triangle that has arisen in their relationship.

Maybe I am also in love with her, or maybe I want her because you want her?

What attracts you to her?

She's beautiful, open, kind, clean. And you are smart, cruel, funny and you are a first-class bitch.

Together, you are the perfect woman.

Do you think you can love two people at the same time? What we want will never happen.

The world will not allow this.

But the world cannot stop us!

Franklin Waugh recalls how in his childhood at a school lesson, he heard a fairy tale about a princess that was tormented by a dilemma. Two men sought her hand in marriage, but she could choose only one of them. Little Franklin could not understand why she could not marry both of them.

And this, as is now clear, was not just the idle curiosity of a child. Until today, he has never been in a relationship with a single partner. "I never had a monogamous relationship in my life," he says. "I came to the school graduation ball with two girls, and I lost my virginity during a threesome. "Now he lives in the same house with his constant partner and her other boyfriend. Sometimes they have a teenage daughter visiting his lover. In addition, he maintains long distance relationships with four other girls. With some of them he meets more often, with others less often.

Franklin and his girls are polyamorous. Their like-minded people prefer to call themselves simply "poly." It is possible that in the future we may begin to look at love relationships in a completely different way and abandon our present ideas about them. And it's not just about sex, but about true love. Your girlfriend has another loved one, and not just one. And you, too, can go on dates, have sex and spend time with anyone you want. And you regularly discuss it. At the same time, you love each other, give birth to children, communicate a lot, and feel happy. Savagery? Lechery? Immorality? Some may agree, but not all. Many will disagree with you. But the "polyamory" has made it possible to have relationships with several partners at once. And no, this is not polygamy — unlike it, the main thing in polyamory is complete trust in your partners, lack of secrets about other relationships and constant communication. [16]

What kind of relationship is this, how to negotiate with your partner, how to cope with jealousy and pressure from a monogamous society?

Beth, 32

I learned about the wonderful phenomenon of "polyamory" a little more than three years ago. I met a couple of polyamors. I absolutely did not like how they build their relationships, but the idea was interesting. It turns out that you can agree with your loved one, communicate openly and honestly, say that you still like someone, that you still have feelings for someone else. When I decided to try and practice polyamory, I perceived myself as the main person in these relationships, and the other partners of my man as secondary. I had the right to choose, to set the rules. But with each new acquaintance with those "side" partners of my partner, I realized that it was wrong to consider other people as "spare." They are people just like me, with their own important values and experiences. There is also a "don't ask, don't tell" kind of relationship. This is similar to the relationship between husband and wife, who have several lovers, they both know about it, but pretend that they are not. I tried this format and thought — why I do not want to know where is my partner and whom he is meeting now? Probably because it will hurt me.

I began to delve into myself and realized that I just want attention. And if he is away, then I will not be bothered by the fact that my partner gives this attention to other people, including sexual and romantic. In general, it is very interesting to discuss the details, it can even be useful. It becomes so wild sometimes, especially for the first time, to discuss his dates, emotions and feelings he experienced, his first kiss with another girl, and his sex... These are such touching moments — it's kind of not customary to talk about it, it seems to be painful, but on the other hand, a person openly shares this with you. This is a very high level of intimacy and it's great.

Polyamory is not mentioned in any census questionnaire, but according to official figures, this phenomenon is becoming more and more widespread.

Some even call for legislative recognition of the rights of polyamorous people, following the legalization of same-sex marriage in the UK and the USA.

The term "polyamory" appeared in the 1990s. The phenomenon of such views on relationships is discussed in an article "*A Bouquet of Lovers*" in 1990. This is one of the first references to "polyamores".Polyamorous partners don't need one-night stand sex. They experience love and emotional affection and are ready to be next to each other in joy and sorrow. [17]

Monogamy is surrounded by a halo of holiness, and those who deviate from this norm are condemned. "Even people in non-monogamous relationships consider monogamous relationships to be better. They have come to terms with the fact that their relationship model is not the best, and it's sad."

The problem is that these labels affect not only polyamorous adults, but also their children.

Maria Pallotta-Chiarolly of Deakin University, Australia, conducted a large-scale study of the lives of children in polyamorous families. What excites her most is what she called the "failure model." This means that outsiders are confident that such a lifestyle of parents negatively affects children, although this is far from being true.

"Scientific research shows that children who grow up in families with many adults are really happy, and they really like it," says Pallotta-Chiarolly. The more adults care for them, the more support and attention children receive.

"These children are more insightful and intelligent; they are open to understanding the diversity and multiple forms of religion and culture. Children see their parents go to work, look after someone who is sick, cook food," she continues. "They see all aspects of family life, but many people thinks that polyamory is just an endless orgy, and children suffer from this kind of life."

This does not mean that all polyamorous families are ideal - they face the same difficulties as any regular family.

There is a striking contradiction. Leading media practically recognize extramarital affairs as a social norm. "But when it comes to ethical non-monogamous relationships... it's considered abnormal" [1] Many poly-activists say that it is inherent in human nature. For them, this is a natural way of life. If this is true, these groups should be protected by law from discrimination, they say.

However, even the polyamores themselves sometimes have doubts about their way of living. In a small study conducted in 2005 by Meg-John Barker of the Open University in the UK, 30 people practicing polyamory were interviewed. When asked about self-identification, only half of them answered that polyamory was "a clear belonging to a certain type of personality" for them, while the remaining half called it "an ethical alternative to infidelity." [1]

Alex, 34

Love is not a hierarchical or finite volume. Love is endless. Polyamory is beautiful and wonderful, for it provides an opportunity for unconditional love. On the other hand, monogamy, most often, implies conditional love. That is, I love you if you fit a certain portrait. You can even hear: "I love you, but I can't accept it because you got better, so I'm sorry, I'm thinner or I don't love you." And in polyamory they love just a person. When we talk about unconditional love, this resource is endless and there can be enough of love for any number of people. Why do not we limit how much love we can give to friends, how many children can we have, but we limit the number of partners for love? This love is all the same, just slightly different ways of experiencing and expressing love.

What are the downsides?

Beth, 32

Lack of time. Suppose you have two or three partners, while still having work, business trips, hobbies, something else, and 24 hours is just not enough. Everyone wants to spend some time with you, and it doesn't work out. And speaking about logistics... If two people live together and have extra partners, you need to somehow understand how to arrange your meetings so that everyone is comfortable. On the financial side, it could also become quite expensive, because if you consciously approach your health, and this is done in my environment, many people need to have been checked on a regular basis. And these medical checks cost money. And these checks need to be done much more often as compared to people who are in monogamous relationships, ideally once every few months, at least you need to have a general examination once in a six months. And it would be nice to have money for a psychotherapist, because psychologically it's still difficult, at least because it is not accepted generally. You are brought up in a certain framework, from which you need to go, feel and understand what you want. Often it is difficult for people to handle all this job of understanding by themselves.

Any relationship conceals pitfalls.

And if it's difficult to maintain polyamorous relations, and in addition to the pleasures multiplied by several times, the degree of responsibility, mutual understanding, maturity, and possibly painful moments are doubled or triplicated, then you can choose not so deep, but no less surprising relations.

Chapter 4
Open Marriage:
Other Types of Open Relationships

From our ancestors living in a strictly patriarchal society, we got a superficial look at open relationships. People practicing this type of relationship have to wade through condemnation, and rejection by society. But this same society will cease to be bright in its diversity, as if the palette of colors of Van Gogh has become black and white.

An open relationship is an alliance between two people in which both want to be together, but also want or do not deny the possibility of a relationship (both sexual and romantic) with other partners outside of the couple. This union is built exclusively by mutual agreement. Everyone has the same rights, agreed to in advance. Partners and lovers in such relationships can be of any sexual orientation.

The most important thing is to understand that these free relations are not immoral, "illegal" infidelities; nor are they about permissiveness or promiscuity. Genuine open relationships can exist if there is mutual respect and absolute awareness. Their consequence is total honesty.

Honesty must be the basis of an open relationship. An open relationship should be open and naked, totally, to every unpleasant detail. Only in this way will they work for the mutual good. It is also important to remember the fine line between freedom and the fear of responsibility, between awareness and vanity. It is easy to assert your maturity and awareness in words. In fact, everything will fall into place. The practice of free love will help to understand where are strong and close relationships, and where is an empty bubble.

Linda, 44 years old, interior designer

At forty-four, after seventeen years of marriage, having raised three children, I discovered sex. This sex was not with my husband.

No, I love him, respect him and never regretted marrying him. We are an excellent team and we always find a common language in all the basic family matters: spend money on diamonds or a car, go on vacation to the Maldives or on a weekend in Monaco. My husband, an investment banker, is successful and handsome. No one in my life made me laugh like he did, and I never met a man wiser.

But we have been married long enough. About eight years ago, I found out that my husband had an affair on the side. I started to have paranoia. I wanted to know who she was, what they were doing, what it all would eventually spill over into. We did not think to get divorced. But the way out of the situation was not found immediately. Still, I remember perfectly the moment when he was discovered. One day, Albert — let it be the name of my husband for the sake of this story — once again did not come home from work. I felt that he was with his mistress, although before that he had promised me not to meet her again. In general, that evening the monthly supply of Veuve Clicquot in our wine cabinet ran out. When the time had come for a "Bloody Mary",

I had an insight: I cannot control the life of my husband. The only person in my control is myself (well, well, at that moment I was rather under control of that "Bloody Mary").

The next morning, I decided to concentrate on what I want. Most important to me were our children. The youngest was in the second grade and lived with us. The two older children had long been sent to an English boarding house, but at that moment they were at home on vacation. Spending the summer and a couple of the best years of their life while watching their parents trying to set their personal relationships straight is not the best dream of a teenager. Let the children continue to think that the midlife crisis is when dad buys "Ferrari" and mom, a plasma therapy course, that's all.

When discussing with Albert how we will continue to live, we always tried to hide marriage issues from our children. The next priority was our ambition. Albert masterfully juggled derivatives, I was a master of decorating villas first in Saint-Tropez, and then everywhere else. Domenico and Stefano met us at the Alta Moda show as relatives, our cards of the 418 Club members were the first distribution. Of course, Tatler wrote about us, and we liked it all. We wanted our marriage to help us continue to live this lifestyle, and there was no tragedy in the fact that we slept in different bedrooms. We agreed that we will not make a divorce because of relations on the side. That new love or new sex is the same joys of family life as the first of September in the Kaptsov gymnasium or the first of January in Courchevel.

I will not say that Albert and I immediately agreed on everything. For starters, I stopped interrogating him, he did the same with me. Sometimes we even discussed our lovers. We wanted to be as honest with each other as possible. People call such unions open marriage. But I hate this term. The word "open" gives the impression that I am glad for any stranger in his bed. In fact, I approach the choice of lovers even more carefully than the choice of birds on de Gournay wallpapers for my clients, and I am sure Albert also deals with venture capital investments only at work.

But to become free in our forties and fifties is wonderful. They say scientists recently found that middle-aged women enjoy sex more than women in their twenties or thirties. And it is true. Moreover, I know for sure that I could not get all the joy from sex that I get now if I had one and only partner.

We, the people of the 21st century, consider ourselves smart. But at the same time, we continue to believe in fairy tales about Meghan

Markle – that the one and only prince is waiting for us somewhere, and we will be forever happy with him. But love is a temporary, fleeting state. The fairy tale always fades away eventually, and is replaced by everyday love, mundane love which is the basis of any long-term relationship. Over the past few years, I learned a lot about myself. For example, that I can be in love with two men at once. That I'm much more cheerful than I always thought. That a romance at fifty is no worse than a romance at thirty. What is most important in others is not how they behave when you are not together, but what they do when you are near. I am no longer jealous - perhaps because now I clearly understand my role in the life of my men.

The downside is that none of my men can be called mine. The plus is that none of them can call me their own. I am an independent woman and as free as possible, to the extent that this freedom does not negatively affect the lives of my children.

Romances, it turns out, end as easily as they begin. Parting is always sad. And although I never focused on finding the next partner, I am always open for new relationships - and it helps.

Sex in my marriage may reappear one day. My husband and I still spend vacations with our children on the beaches of Pampelonne and Augustus, we go together to Dmitry Chernyakov in Paris, to Ilya Kabakov in London, to the celery root in Copenhagen. By admitting that we cannot be everything to each other, we got rid of unnecessary pressure and now we try to be what we can be.

We still like each other, admire each other, and we are still interested in spending time together. Among our friends there are many who opened that Pandora's box called "divorce" instead of opening the "widow" box and agreeing that the only third extra in their marriage is Dobrovinsky's lawyer. Others, gritting their teeth, stay together at least for the sake of the Tatler Ball. Some completely desperate spouses hide their mistresses in hotels in Sardinia no less thoroughly than their offshore accounts. This kind of joy in the end leads only to the hospital ward or to the surgical operating room for treatment of heart diseases.

My marriage is not perfect either. But now, when I stopped endlessly thinking about what an ideal marriage should be like, I'm sure we will have a long, happy family life.

Shannon, 27, buyer

"I don't believe in monogamy," fashion architect Alex told me on a first date. If the husband is faithful, then he is porn addicted. Instead of watching porn, it's better to have sex with real people. You girls have been lying about princes since childhood." "What an interesting man!" I thought. "But I don't need such a boyfriend." A month later we met again.

Alex always had several partners at once before our relationship started; but for a whole year while we were together there was no one else but me. And after a year, he started to attend nightclubs frequently — again. "I love you more than anyone," he said. "And you only have yourself to blame for not being able to accept me as I am."

It was my decision to offer him an open relationship. I thought that it would be better to have him by my side from time to time than don´t have him at all. We have read several books on the psychology of marriage. "Discuss the boundaries of your relationship," it was written in them. "Respect the partner's fears, be honest." We talked about what attracted his girls. It turned out that if I can't accept something, then first of all I will talk about the beauty of someone else's breast. I made a huge list of rules.

"Tell me if you are dating a girl today." "Call me when you meet." "Call after you leave her." "Spend the nights at home."

Once Alex was on a business trip. I went to have some croissants for breakfast at Remy Kitchen Bakery. There was a pretty hostess. An equally attractive girl was sitting at a table and eating her avocado salad. And I realized that I was thinking: if Alex was with me right now, I would, without looking at him, know where he is currently looking to. And I started to cry. I have realized that I was tired of constant competition with all the women in this world. I grew tired of believing that others seem attractive to him just because they are not me.

We came up with new rules - the same for both. And then agreed to part, but from time to time spend a week together. I finally started to have relationships with other men. Every Monday, Alex and I met to discuss our feelings and sensations.

And then I slept with his colleague from the architectural bureau. It was just sex for me, but it made Alex jealous. He said that we did not agree to sleep with friends and, in general, he felt "stuck" in our relationship. It was clear to me: he was not even ready to admit the thought that someone other than him would become more than just a lover to me. And to tolerate the same disrespectful attitude as in ordinary relationship while being in open one... well, this is the highest degree of masochism I can think about. To make this possible, the tyrant should at least have the face, body and bank account of Christian Gray.

I finally admitted to myself that all this time I was deceiving myself. I cannot close my eyes to his betrayal. And I do not need a relationship with such a distance. And so we broke up with him.

Free relations taught me to empathize. Now I'm more confident in myself, because from the very beginning of a new love affair I define boundaries that I'm not ready to cross myself and which I won't let my partner cross as well. Your freedom in relationships, as in everything else, ends where the freedom of another person begins.

Open relationships can reveal all the cards. They will demonstrate where there is love and respect, and where there are lies and deceit. This type of relationship may become a temporary measure on the way to either a final separation or returning to the previous rules. Open relationship can save and maintain unity of a couple during a crisis. You can try it when it seems that love has withered away. And often it may indeed seem that if you don't want to end in ruins of your love it is better to give each other more freedom in order to understand the value and significance of the relationship you are in.

People are often confused about the terms. Such misconceptions are confusing, could interfere with grasping the fine details and intricacies of your feelings. This subsequently leads to a blind denial of open relationships.

• Love and chemistry of love are different phenomena. They have the opposite nature. Chemistry of love is momentary and frivolous. It is based on passion, on sexual arousal. Love, when it is genuine, conscious, does not necessarily embody sexual, romantic and emotional relationships. Chemistry of love often, but not necessarily always, begins with falling in love. But not each and every chemistry of love grows into love. Taking this difference as a reference point in the coordinated system of relationships, we can conclude that free relations are an opportunity to maintain a union of partners with a momentary enthusiasm, or affair.

• Polyamory and free relations. Polyamory implies the absence of a single design, a pair - there are always more than two partners in a single bunch, each lover is equal. But in a open relationship or in an open marriage, there is only one bunch - a couple who has secondary connections on the side.

• Promiscuity and free relations. Some, through their ignorance, may confuse promiscuity, promiscuous sex with an open relationship, or open marriage with free relations. And this is fundamental mistake. Promiscuity does not have a single restriction or rules in terms of sex, while free relations are built solely on agreed terms and conditions. Anyway, promiscuity is exclusively about the sexual contacts, and an open relationship is not only about sex, but also about flirting, and emotional proximity.

People in a couple are often connected not only by love, but also by the similarity of mindsets and opinions, by a common cause, by a common way and style of life, a common circle of friends and relatives, and sometimes by children. For example, a pair of vegans — it's convenient for them to live and build life together. Childfree — they are on the same page. A general startup — a project that can fall apart if the couple separates. Well, when it comes to children, then arguments are not required here — you need to try and keep the marriage or relationship, and you can't leave hastily. Therefore, free relations not only add more diversity, sometimes this is the only way to save the union, the family.

Let's see what the **advantages of an open relationship** are:

• You can escape boredom. Relationships become less boring and more varied, a sexual attraction that had faded could return. Interest in each other is growing. Now both partners are free to live as they like.

• Forbidden fruit is sweet. But when there is no restrictions, the desire to taste it fades.

• A clear conscience. The absurd obligations that existed because of the fear of misunderstanding and understatement are reduced. Any connections on the side, not necessarily sexual, harmless flirting, and dating are now not secret, they are out in the open and permitted.

• Self-sufficiency. Many couples are very dependent on each other, have a strong affection. However, this is a painful and destructive condition. We tend to love and desire a person that is self-sufficient, and not relying constantly on others.

• Less pain or no pain at all. If open relationships are built on exceptional awareness, as ideally they should be, then the pain of jealousy no longer scorches your hearts. After all, everything is under control within the boundaries which you have both agreed on.

A well-known Russian politician and publicist, 62-year-old Irina Khakamada admitted in an interview that she has been living with her husband Vladimir Sirotinsky in a free marriage for a long time [18]

> "We concluded a non-aggression pact, coexistence, since we are wildly interesting to each other, and about freedom. We have partnerships," explained the publicist in a video interview. We are two persons of considerable age. And we are not interested in being with one person all the time, it bothers us. That's all. We agreed on this on the third year of communication." Khakamada and Sirotinsky have been married for more than 20 years.

In another interview, she made a reservation on the same topic with a phrase as a disclaimer for listeners "Such relationships require a high level of awareness. And if you are not confident in yourself, please do not try and implement our experience in your life."

The **disadvantages of open relationships**, and to whom they will not fit

Like it or not, there are few who are really ready for an open relationship. This kind of relationship has many pitfalls. Key disadvantages of free relations are:

• Quiet jealousy. You can agree on everything, but the slightest surge of emotions, and emotions and feelings like jealousy, a feeling of abandonment, uselessness — they all could wake up. So, the relationship in a couple can only get worse.

• Separation from each other. During an open relationship, a certain kind of alienation may arise between partners. This may be temporary, but it will affect relations within the union.

• Condemnation by society. No matter how we imagine society — tolerant, accepting any position in life — the majority will condemn free relations. We can tell it even without showing any statistics. Just think about possible reactions from your parents, colleagues, and friends. Surely at least some, if not the majority of them, will disapprove.

• Unpleasant consequences. External connections may be unsuccessful, which will bring unnecessary worries and troubles not only to you, but also to your partner. Among such consequences could be, for example, sexually transmitted diseases or an unplanned pregnancy of the side partner.

• It is difficult to find a partner on the side. Few will be happy with this prospect: easy flirtation and sex for one night. Many want to be the one and only. Few want to be just another someone of hundreds, everyone imagine themselves to be special.

From the point of view of science

Sexologists know that in partners who are in a long-term relationship, passion and sexual desire gradually decrease. [19] Relations in a couple become closer, family, there is a little uncharted territory remains, and everything is well-known as partners have observed each other over long time in various situations. In turn, sexual attraction is based on a certain degree of prohibition, secrecy and inaccessibility. And just the same, when a close, beloved partner ceases to be that inaccessible and impossible to reach, passion fades away. Open relationships can help reignite that faded passion. However, this is not the only way, and certainly not the most successful for most.

There are many other ways. It all depends on the personality. Often only one partner needs free relations, and the other has to adjust, which can also play a cruel joke on both in the long run. Perhaps your case is individual, or unpredictable reasons and incentives are hidden behind the desire for an open relationship. It is better to consult a therapist first. Not to mention internal problems, such relationships also bring a lot of difficult moments to life outside your couple. Society hardly accepts things that cannot be told openly to children or parents. In the next chapter, we will try to understand why society rejects open relations and how to deal with it.

Chapter 5
Social Rejection: Causes and Explanations

The attitude of society towards polyamory is not always positive. There are many prejudices about polyamorous relationships, and one of the most common is that they are based solely on sex. The fact of having several partners at the same time is often associated with a dissolute lifestyle. Any problems that have arisen in a monogamous family — poor school performance of children at school, illness, financial troubles, and addictions, — society will perceive ambivalently: some will sympathize, and some will try to find an excuse to put the blame. And if polyamorist people face the same problems, most people from the same society will attribute all the problems to one, main reason — in their opinion, is non-monogamy!

Polyamoria is subjected to strong stigmatization - to some extent stronger than any gender, race, class, religion, political attitude or sexual orientation. Conservative and religious people are especially hostile towards polyamory. The political status of polyamory is comparable to the status of homosexuality before the Stonewall riots in 1969, which marked the beginning of the gay rights movement [20]

It is important to keep in mind that the societies that managed to become major technological civilizations were those that adopted monogamous marriage as the gold standard for long-term pairing and family formation.

Of course, married people often had affairs, men visited prostitutes, and elites were often polygynous or polyamorous even when they propagated monogamy in public. But monogamy has historically and normatively been central to complex societies.

Monogamy has reduced the spread of sexually transmitted diseases (STD) that can undermine the fertility of women. However, STDs have become much less common over the past few centuries. STDs are now easier to avoid with vaccines, condoms, and safer sex, and they are easier to treat with drugs developed in 20th century.

Perhaps most importantly, monogamy has reduced the ability of men with high status to monopolize women and helped equalize mating opportunities. This has reduced violent competition among men.

Why are polyamorous families worse? Perhaps the future lies with them? The truth is that it will be difficult to legalize polyamorous marriages, partly because there are many varieties of polyamorous relationships. All polyamorous families are different.

On the other hand, it would seem that there are no obstacles to the official registration of polyamorous marriages in the event that all partners live under one roof and have no additional relations on the side.

How can this be done? Parental obligations and ownership rights to real estate may be determined by law. In addition, biological kinship between those who marry and the children they will raise can be taken into account.

Of course, difficulties cannot be avoided, but they are largely similar to the challenges faced by those who want to adopt a child. The situation may be complicated by relations on the side, however, there are similar legal solutions for divorce and custody of children.

The main problem for polyamors today is the lack of legal protection - for example, the absence of laws that prevent discrimination.

For example, under the US Army Code of War cheating is considered a crime, and those who are legally married cannot practice polyamory openly. [1]

To legislatively protect polyamory, first it must be recognized as a sexual orientation, as is homosexuality.

If the law recognizing polyamory as orientation is adopted, the polyamory partners will be protected by similar anti-discrimination laws.

Anne Tweedy, lawyer from Hamline University, had recently made her case for considering polyamory an orientation. She says that sexual orientation is defined as an attraction to members of one's gender, the opposite sex, or both sexes. [1]

The field of law believes that polyamory can be considered a sexual orientation if it is an integral part of a person's personality. [1]

However, other sexual preferences, which are an integral part of the personality of a particular person, can be included into this concept.

Kathryn, 24

> "If you are a polyamor, many people think that
> all you do is just fucking. I really respect pcoplc

who speak about their views and preferences in advance, before date. Just in the context of the conversation, you say that you have non-standard views. Of course, very often condemnations sound in response, something like: "You will rethink it later," "You just haven't had your fill yet," "Oh, you fucking did," and so on. Recently, I was just in such a relationship, they immediately told me that everything is perfect, and suits them well, and everything is cool. And somehow we sat down, had a good drink together and it all started: "When will you change your mind?", "Aren't you sick with everything you can do," "You haven't got real love." Another misconception that I often hear when meeting someone: "It's cool that you are a polyamor, I'm just not looking for a serious relationship." In the case of polyamory, this is just about a serious relationship, and not about just getting laid. Unfortunately, polyamory is becoming mainstream, it's cool to call yourself polyamory even if it's not about you. For some reason, no one remembers that polyamorous relationship is about honesty, ethics, agreed-upon boundaries, and openness, but they remember that you can have sex with several people and calmly tell your girlfriend that she's not the only one, revealing that you are not truly interested in how she feels. It is very sad that this is becoming fashionable. I'm probably lucky, no matter how rude it sounds — I don't communicate with my parents. If I had told to my religious family at first about my passion for BDSM, and then about polyamory – I would have been burned at the stake.

Such "scandalous" innovations always go through a very serious struggle in society in all social spheres - legal, psychological, cultural. A certain critical mass of examples of this form of relations should accumulate, such as documentary films and feature films, pop culture products, and literary works. The new image is first recorded in the minds of people through the media. And only after a while, the collective unconscious will be able to accept a new form of family and relationships.

Many Western conservatives believe that monogamy is the foundation of Western civilization, and any threat to monogamy is the threat to love, marriage, culture, the nation and the gene pool of the nation as well.

Polyamory is almost invisible in the mainstream media. Most doctors, psychotherapists, and mental health professionals are unaware of polyamory, and many of them are biased toward mono-relationships, so they do not really help non-monogamous people who seek professional help.

Many specialists are poorly informed about the particularities of lifestyle and specific needs of polyamorous people, and most textbooks and brochures on psychology and psychotherapy do not mention this form of relationship. Among the few works that focus on psychotherapy for polyamorous clients, we can mention the earliest publication by Hymer & Rubin (1982), the works of Weitzman (2006) and Labriola (2013).

The present is a time of dramatic social and cultural changes. People are on the verge of a new world order. A huge number of new trends break into everyday life, and these trends literally reshape our mentality. Economy, technology, community structure, lifestyle and opportunities are changing, the way of thinking is changing, and today it is a global process. If you feel that the direction of polyamory is your inclination, do not be afraid to study, learn, feel, and wonder. And if you are a supporter of centuries-old traditional relationships in marriage, try not to blame people practicing other forms of relationships. The world is diverse. There is a place in it for everyone. And only the criterion "do no harm to yourself and others" is a true assessment of what is good and what is bad.

Everyone is on their own way, and let´s everyone choose their own way, direction and company for this journey, guided not by hate, or fear, or disdain, but exclusively by love.

Chapter 6
Polyamory in History, Literature and Cinema

In History

You will be surprised when you find out how many famous people have experienced polyamorous relationships. Where there is freedom, there will be a choice. And freedom is the privilege of people of creativity and power. If you possess inner freedom, you are able to create an extraordinary story of love and sexual incarnations in your own life. Here are some interesting facts about love and the love affairs of famous people in history.

Caligula, the famous ruler of the Ancient Rome, was very passionate and well-known for his numerous love affairs. He even had a special passion for his four-legged friend - a stallion. He was not suspected of bestiality, however. His love for the horse brought the stallion to the Senate at the behest of the ruler. Caligula loved only one man more than his horse: that man was his uterine brother. The famous film of the same name, *Tinto Brass*, with McDowell in the title role, also narrates this story. And Caligula ended badly – Roman nobles killed him. [21]

Louis the Fifteenth surpassed in the joys of all the other French monarchs, even the famous King's son, Louis the Fourteenth. His famous love passion was Madame Marquise de Pompadour. She was a rather depraved lady, while not jealous at all. Therefore, His Majesty managed to maintain, in addition to her, a whole park called *Deer*. In this park, in separate houses, royal mistresses of the heart lived, catering to cravings of His Royal Majesty [21]

It's no secret that the most successful and most famous in love affairs is Mr. Giacomo Casanova. His fame preceded him wherever he appeared. Still, he was also considered the most brilliant, successful and loving. So, he made it into history as such. And despite the fact that he was adored by all the female representatives, Mr.

Casanova died in poverty, poor and completely alone. He paid that price for love.

The Marquis de Sade was not at all as bloodthirsty as his stories describe. Of course, sadism was present in his practice, which was spread precisely from him. He laid the foundation for whipping, and for that practice he served in psychiatric hospitals and even in prisons in many regions of France. That is while serving his sentences he wrote many books, which are recommended for reading only after reaching twenty-one years (Secret History Isabella Bavaria , Zhyustina, Crimes love or passion Follies, Marquise de Ganges...)

Catherine II had her most cherished favorite — count Grigoriy Orlov.

Jimmy Hendrix has surpassed all known ladies' men. In just twenty-eight years of his life he recorded in his history more than one thousand lucky women with whom he had sex! [22]

Charlie Chaplin had a special addiction to "nymphet," that is, to very young girls. Moreover, his passion reached the point that he married them. In this regard, he was constantly condemned by the public. However, like any celebrity, he got away with it [23]

The story of poet Vladimir Mayakovsky and his love Lily Brik. By the time of the meeting with Mayakovsky, Lily was already married to Osip Brik. Their house was s popular meeting place for artists, poets, and politicians. In 1915, Lily's sister Elsa introduced Brik couple to her close friend and admirer, budding poet Vladimir Mayakovsky, with whom she wanted to connect her future life. He accepted this invitation, attended the gathering, and recited his popular poem Cloud in Pants... That very night, as Elsa claims, everything happened: "Briks irrevocably loved Mayakovsky's poems, and Volodya irrevocably fell in love with Lily." A few days later, Mayakovsky urged Briks to accept him for good, explaining his desire by saying that he "fell in love with Lilya Yuryevna." She gave her consent, and Osip was forced to put up with the whims of his giddy wife. Thus, began one of the high-profile stories of the past century, the "three-way marriage," rumors of which were quickly spreading in literary circles. And although Lily explained to everyone that "with Axes, she had an intimate relationship long ago," the strange trinity still lived under the same roof.

Virginia Woolf and Vita Sackville West. Both writers were married at the time of their romance. "I really slept with her (twice), but that's all," Vita wrote to her husband. "Now you know about it, and I hope I didn't shock you." Woolf wrote a more genuine love letter to her friend - the Orlando novel.

Such unusual relationships amaze the imagination and become fascinating material for works of literature.

In literature

Ernest Hemingway's *"The Garden of Eden"* (The Garden of Eden, 1986)

During a honeymoon on the Riviera, an American writer and his wife meet a young woman, and both fall in love with her. It is believed that this Hemingway novel is autobiographical.

The Ulysses by James Joyce (Ulysses, 1918)

Leopold Bloom put up with cheating on his wife. Molly can really be understood: she had not had sex with Bloom for ten whole years.

"The Handmaid's Tale" by Margaret Atwood (The Handmaid's Tale, 1885)

In the fictional republic of Gilead, there is a special caste of women whom infertile couples use as surrogate mothers. The main character, a servant in the house of the Commander and his wife, is required to have sex with him every month. In addition to the book, by the way, now there is a television series, which even received an Emmy award.

Anapol Deborah. *Polyamory in the 21st century: Love and intimacy with multiple partners.* Lanham, MA: Rowman & Littlefield Pub., 2012.

The central thesis of Deborah Anapol is that polyamoria is natural and widespread in society. However, she speaks of it as an institution of betrayal, workplace romances, suppressed desires and languid memories of a happy youth, where monogamy is minimized. The only question this book explores is how to overcome the norms blocking one's own sexual identity. Easton D. The Ethical Slut: Gayatri Publishing House, 1997

Dossy Easton and Catherine Liszt construct an ethic of bodily love without limits. They show from their own experience that one can live surprisingly easily and carelessly, falling in love with those whom one wants to fall in love with, and leaving those to whom the attraction fades away. The book is written in the genre of justification of personal sexual drives and practical recommendations for those who want to follow the example of love without restrictions.

Veaux F., Rickert E. *More than two: A practical guide to ethical polyamory* / Foreword by J.W. Hardy Portland: Torontree Press, 2014

The book presents more than thirty years of the main character, Franklin Wow's, polyamory experience, who started blogging about his sexual performances in 1997, at the same time as the publication of Dossy Easton and Catherine List Eva Rickert with her husband ceased to practice monogamy in a relationship much later, in 2008. But, as noted in the book, Eve first became familiar with the concept of polyamory at age 12 in biology classes, when the teacher explained the characteristics of primary and secondary sexual partners. Later there was the experience of open relations at college, and finally, a mutual decision with her spouse about the only way to continue living together without lies and deceit - the removal of any restrictions on marital fidelity.

Labriola K. *The jealousy workbook: Exercises and insights for managing open relationships.* Berkeley, CA: Greenery Press, 2013

Family consultant Katie Labriola pays particular attention to jealousy as the main negative psychological experience associated with open relationships. The book is built as a guide to overcome the negative consequences of adultery. The book is divided into two parts. In the first, jealousy as a socially conditioned emotion is examined in detail. The second part is about the free change of partners, as a conscious choice, and not a violation of morality.

Ed. by E. Sheff. *Stories from the polycule: Real life in polyamorous families* / Portland: Torontree Press, 2015

Elizabeth Chef has compiled a collection of stories of people living in polyamorous families; stories recorded by author tell about fate and feelings of those people, their assessments of the past and ideas about the future. The age of storytellers whose stories were included in the collection ranges from five to fifty-five years. This removes the exclusively sexual background of polyamorous relationships. The child is more likely to talk about his perception of life in an unusual and, at first glance, completely unacceptable situation.

The collection contains stories about the very first impressions of polyamorous relationships, fractures of fate, when people entered into a situation of multiple sexual relations as a result of their own choice or choice of their partner.

On the screen

"Sex of Angels", dir. H. Villaverde, 2002

Charming Spanish romance with the beauty Astrid Berger Frisbee in the lead role. Her heroine Carla is dating a beautiful young man. But suddenly the boyfriend feels attracted to the dancer Ray, and the couple breaks up. But Carla won't give up so easily: first, she wins back her boyfriend from her ex, and then three young people come to a decision that satisfies the whole trinity.

Crazy, vulgar and absolutely unparalleled picture with Gerard Depardieu, Jeanne Moreau, Isabelle Huppert, Patrick Dever and Miu-Miu. Two rebels steal a car from a hairdresser. Together with the car, his woman is at their disposal. The three of them have sex and romp around France, hiding from the police.

"Prepare Your Handkerchiefs," dir. B. Blie, 1977

Another film of the rebel-esthete Blie, which had also won him an Oscar. Starring, by the way, again Gerard Depardieu and Patrick Dever. Raoul, tired of Solange's eternal depression, invites a casual man in a restaurant to become her lover. Maybe then the woman will feel better. But Solange wants something completely different.

"Etudes of the Three", dir. S. G. Ruiz, 2009

The melodrama about the Madrid students of the art faculty, who made three of them love, is true, for physiological reasons. But soon love was superimposed on sex. Overly mannered, the film now and then changes emphasis: it turns into a story about relationships, sometimes it demonstrates the contrast and opposition between the poor artist and the rich one, at the other moment the movie focuses on talent vs mediocrity opposition.

"Jules and Jim", dir. F. Truffaut, 1962

The great film by Francois Truffaut, dedicated to the love of the three, ends tragically. For the leading heroes, inseparable Jules and Jim, these relationships were not a whim, but a way of survival; and the fatal Catherine performed by the incredible Jeanne Moreau puts an end to the painful relationship of inseparable friends.

"Third Meshchanskaya", dir. A. Room, 1927

In the story of how a man named Vladimir settled in the apartment of a married couple and after a while they began to live together, the beloved "poet with at least a small but graceful strength" (large, of course) can easily be guessed by everyone.

The idea to make a film based on real events came up with the scandalous literary critic Viktor Shklovsky, who turned himself into a screenwriter in the late 1920s. Fortunately, there were more than enough ideas and plots around. But there was less time left for free implementation of these plots and ideas.

"Being John Malkovich", dir. S. Jones, 1999

This crazy story from screenwriter Charlie Kaufman
tells us about how a simple archivist, working on the
seventh and a half floor, discovered the door to the
head of the artist John Malkovich.

Of course, the main point of interest of this film is not
some sexual fantasies. But neither have they played
the last part, otherwise the picture would end
differently. The three main characters are responsible
for a unique scene of a kind with the sultry special
Maxine, Malkovich and the girl Lotte, who at the time
of intimacy was in Malkovich's head.

"Our Time", dir. C. Reygadas, 2018

Mexican drama takes place on farmers' spaces. Juan, a middle-aged man with a good career and a big house, not only does not condemn the beautiful wife for having an affair with an American horse trainer, but even consciously adjusts her violent sex with friends. All so that passion does not go out. The main roles of Juan and his wife were played by the director himself and his real wife.

"Imaginary Love", dir. C. Dolan, 2010

The second and in some respects the most successful film of the Canadian movie director Xavier Dolan.

Two hipsters, gay Francis and vintage enthusiast Marie, gracefully compete for a curly-haired handsome man: quotes from Araki and Audrey Hepburn will be used. But when the handsome man gets tired of all this whistle, he will quickly find an impressive replacement.

"Love of Lions", dir. A. Warda, 1970

The Franco-Belgian director left for Hollywood and, among other things, shot the hippie manifesto: lively, funny, daring. Three shaggy red actors dream of popularity, drink, make love, swim in the pool and create art objects from their bodies. All this time a movie is being made about them.

"Zed and Two Zeros", dir. P. Greenway, 1985

As usual with the British artist Greenaway, sex and death are intertwined in this film in a very ornamental interaction. The plot of the picture is built around twin brothers, zoologists, whose wives died in a car accident. Then the men decide to experimentally observe what happens to the flesh after death, and at the same time make love to the mother of the deceased women.

"Drama", dir. M. Lear, 2010

Again, a trinity of students from the world of art, only now not artists, but theater-goers. Impressed by the teacher's stories about Antonin Artaud, they decide to take his commandments into service and turn their life into a pagan representation, and their bodies into an instrument and decoration.

"Difficult Children", dir. J.-P. Melville, 1950

The novel of the same name by Jean Cocteau and the film shot under his compulsive guidance finally cemented the expression "winged terrible".

The story of rich, aristocratic and eccentric brothers and sisters living without parents and taking boy Gerard under their wing formed the basis of the future novel Dreamers and added incestuous dressing to many French-speaking conversations about brothers and sisters

"Cold Shower", dir. A. Cordier, 2005

The debut full length film of an elderly Frenchman is a teenage drama not only in genre, but also in the ability to tell a story. The film switches feverishly between the gyms full of love and the kitchen disputes of parents, and it is hard to understand what the movie is telling us and why.

But credit is due, the theme of men's shower rooms in this picture is explored in minute details.

"Vicky Cristina Barcelona", dir. W. Allen, 2008

Full of romance polygons, the sweet Catalan film of Woody Allen, among other things, will also show menage-a-trois. Characters of Scarlett Johansson, Javier Bardem and Penelope Cruz will first live tightly in one house, but honey spills in the air, and, therefore, love is just around the corner.

"French Twist", dir. J. Balasco, 1994

The comedy, which was nominated for many categories of the Cesar Award, could become a story about a love triangle: a scoundrel husband, a languishing wife, and a cheerful lesbian... if everyone in this arrangement did not change roles here and there. The main role in the film is played by one of Pedro Almodovar's favorites, Victoria Abril.

Luchino Visconti, this Italian follower of Thomas
Mann, completely prevents his heroes from breathing.
The only time they can take a breath of fresh air is the
scene on the balcony of the long-suffering palazzo,
where the whole agitated professor couple will find
themselves. As for the three of love, you can choose
any of the variations. But first of all, we are talking, of
course, about young heroes: Liette, Stefano and the
unforgettable Conrad.

"Dreamers", dir. B. Bertolucci, 2003

Despite Jules and Jim, Waltzes and other classics, it
was Bertolucci who revealed to the mass audience how
much this audience loves movies about love of three
persons. A student revolution can happen, a world war
could start, or nothing can happen, but the trio who
runs around the Louvre, smokes, discusses Buster
Keaton and Jimmy Hendrix, drinks wine and makes
love, and never stops beckoning and seducing.

And the rest of the world is unnecessary and excessive
for them...

"Goodbye", dir. F. Ozone, 2005

It is not easy to choose one film among the works of the scandalous of the French bourgeois directors. Therefore, the drama about the dying photographer looks like a winner.

Ménage-a-trois in *"Farewell Time"* does not stand in the center of the plot, but on the periphery: the protagonist helps the childless couple to find happiness, and for themselves to stay in this world not only with the help of photographs, but also of the heir.

"Three", dir. E. Fleming, 1994

One of the mainstream three-man love films is a student youth romantic comedy with the future heroine of "Twin Peaks" in the lead role (though not Laura, but Donna).

A girl is mistakenly hooked into a room in a male student dormitory. What could become a love triangle with an unfortunate third odd, turned, according to the precepts of the French, into a relationship that knows no boundaries.

"Especially Dangerous", dir. O. Stone, 2012

Crazy crime thriller with two alternative endings from
the madman Oliver Stone unveils a story about a trio
of beautiful Californians who make their quite
comfortable living by growing top-quality weed. They
live near the ocean, around them are dangers and
stupefying vapors of cannabis, so there is little
surprise that from the very beginning the trio choose a
three-way relationship.

Starring — just think of it! — Aaron Taylor-Johnson,
Blake Lively and Taylor Kitsch.

"Luxurious Life", dir. G. Araki, 1999

The rebellious spirit Araki from Los Angeles, who made crazy, bloody, metaphysical travel pictures The Bare Wire and Nowhere, in the late 90s started to explore genre films; and from time to time he creates films where the provocation turns into an accessory, anecdote or an element of parody.

"Luxurious life" is like a spectator melodrama with a popular soundtrack and a glossy picture, only the search for love is not in the pursuit of the one, but in solving the problem of how to keep them all.

"Threesome Love," dir. T. Tykver, 2010

One of the few films about menage-a-trois, where the characters are over 40. The events of the film are unfolding in Berlin. Hannah, over the years tired of marital relations, cheats on her husband with a man named Adam. But soon, Adam will also develop an interest in the spouse who has just survived an unpleasant operation.

Director Tykver seems to be full of fondness for his heroes, but the picture is more satirical than any other. The film, by the way, was nominated for the Golden Lion in Venice.

"Unmade Beds", dir. A. Dos Santos, 2009

In this hipster picture, created by the Chilean director, the story begins and continues in London, and there are more than enough tenderness. Young, handsome, and curly-haired Axel arrives in the English capital in search for his father, and immediately gets acquainted with a nice couple who own a bar, live in a loft, throw parties, organize concerts, and all that jazz. Soon the three of them will be in the same bed, but for Axel it will be more a search for intimacy and community with someone than a sexual experiment.

"Love", dir. G. Noet, 2015

Gaspard Noet, a universal Argentine-French favorite who looks like a drug lord, in 2015 made his old dream come true and made a 3D movie about sex. Surprisingly, this turned out to be a quite sentimental picture: the Parisian director Murphy, the author's alter ego, looks at his wife and dreams of a departed love. These dreams lurk the reasons why the film was banned for Russian distribution.

"The Gang of Outsiders", dir. JL Godard, 1964

Another film cited by Bertolucci is *Dreamers*, one more great work of the "new wave" art. In the local trio there is no obvious sex connotation, and love, but not for nothing that this film works so well with Jules and Jim and Difficult Children. If two men and one beautiful woman are up to something together, an erotic connotation cannot be avoided. If they have a gun, then only God knows how it all ends.

"All songs are only about love", dir. C. Honore, 2007

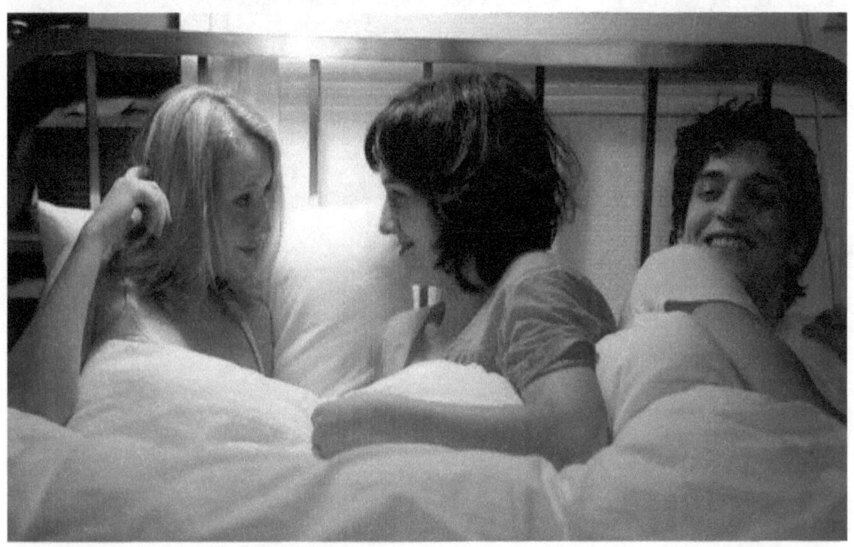

Frenchman Christoph Honore regularly creates films worthy of the Cannes Film Festival, but his all-over-the-world fame begun with this musical. A picture starring Louis Garrell, Ludivin Sagnier and Chiara Mastroiani shows us that nothing lasts forever, and also teaches us about the ease of being, — in both good and bad sense of it.Despite the fact that character of Louis Garrell changes his orientation during the film, he gets married with two girls: the bride Julie and colleague Alice, who helps the couple diversify their relationships. By the way, this film contains a great scene that could be used as example of how to talk with parents about sex in general and about threesome in particular.

A semi-biographical story dedicated to Henry Miller, his wife, and their common lover — memoirist Anais Nin. The action, of course, takes place in the bohemian Paris of the 30s, where the writer and his spouse arrive, having earned scandalous reputation in their homeland. Miller's forbidden books flow into the forbidden pleasures of real life, and Anais quickly forgets that until recently she lacked passions.

"And your mother, too," dir. A. Cuaron, 2001

Mexican summer. Two teenagers cling to the sultry beautiful girl on the beach and offer her to go on a magical journey to another beach, mysterious, but even more beautiful. On the road, they are waiting to get carried away by drugs and pleasure from each other. But in a good movie, sex always goes hand in hand with death.

Infidelity and Jealousy: Recipes to Eliminate It

Infidelity in monogamy

Adultery appeared with the invention of marriage and marital fidelity. Infidelity has the power that marriage can only envy. This power is that great, that the only covenant that is repeated twice in the Bible concerns adultery: once as a ban on adultery per se, and the second on the very thoughts of it. This is not surprising, because still in 9 out of 10 countries, women can be killed if caught in infidelity.

When divorcing, the couples themselves determine the reasons for the divorce. Forty-two percent is tension in moral, psychological, emotional reasons. In addition to alienation in relationships, it is also jealousy or adultery.

Adultery is always associated with many unpleasant things. A person who wants to commit adultery must invent stories about why he or she was late at work, whose lipstick remained on his collar, who accompanied her home, whom he or she called/texted/messaged to, and so on. They are forced to lie, lie more, and lie once again. Obviously, an even larger percentage of divorces/separations is due to the unwillingness and inability of people to understand and respect each other.

Historically, when marriage was an economic undertaking, infidelity threatened our financial security. Now that marriage is primarily a romantic arrangement, infidelity threatens our psychological safety.

Throughout the world, people who have cheated on their spouses have said the same thing: they felt alive at that time. Often they tell stories of the recent loss of death of loved ones. Death and mortality often live in the shadow of infidelity. It is as if a human being is asking him- or herself, what else needs to happen to make me feel alive once again in this life?

The real meaning of adultery is not about the sex, but more about a thirst for attention, in a thirst to feel special and necessary. The fact that you understand that you will never live together with your lover powers this thirst up even more.

A fairly common story happened with Elizabeth, who was always happy in marriage, loved her husband and was afraid to hurt him. She always acted as expected from her. She was a good girl, proper wife, and good mother. But she fell in love with a young arborist who came to uproot a tree in her yard after Hurricane Sandy. He, with his truck and tattoos, was quite the opposite of her husband. But at 47, the love affair of this woman turned into a youth that she never had in her life. When we look for the attention of another person, we are not always turning away from our partner, but rather turning to the other.

It would seem that polyamory removes the issue of adultery, by definition. After all, you are not duty-bound to keep your loyalty to one partner.

What is infidelity in polyamory? In monogamy, infidelity is a violation of an existing tradition, institution. About 80% of monogamous pairs are actually polygamous. Of course, this is wrong and unethical. Formally, many people have a monogamous marriage, but for real they are not in a monogamous relationship.

In polyamory, infidelity is a failure to comply with or a violation of prior agreements or boundaries. The couple sits down and discusses things that can hurt. For example, it doesn't bother you if the partner is sleeping with someone else, but it will be unpleasant for you if he will pay attention to another in your presence.

There are many formats in polyamory, one of them is "don't ask, don't tell" – in other words, do it so that I do not know. How is this different from infidelity? With infidelity, you cut off part of your life from a loved one. You do everything so that he or she doesn't have the slightest idea that you have someone else. In polyamory, you don't cut anything. But here it is important to understand that if you choose the "don't ask, don't tell" format, and suddenly, at some point you ask, then I will tell. This is the responsibility of both. When asking a question, you need to know whether you really want to hear an answer to it.

What about jealousy? Of course, jealousy is often present, but polyamorous relationships allow you to work with it. The antonym of jealousy is compersion. What is jealousy? It's when you feel bad, because the person close to you is happy (when he or she is happy not with you). Compersion means that you are happy when your partner is happy, even if your partner now with someone else and not with you. Without compersion, polyamorous relationship is simply impossible.

Rick, 41.

I had a date, on which I, my wife, our girlfriend and her husband were. It was not a swinging when everything is about simple exchange of partners. In our case, it turned out like this: I had a relationship with my wife, the three of us — me, my wife and our girlfriend. This girl had a relationship with her husband, and he also has a relationship with my wife. But there was no joint relationship and no exchange.

Indeed, there are some people who really do not feel jealousy at all, but such people are rare and precious as showpieces from a museum collection. Fortunately, now there is a lot of information on how to deal with jealousy. Basically, these are therapeutic methods — you sit down and you talk it through.

First of all, honestly admit that you are jealous. This concept itself may include a lack of attention, low self-esteem, or something else, and you need to get to what really bothers you. Maybe the issue is with the partner? Maybe he or she behaves in a way that hurts you? Maybe the question is in you, in your visions. The most important thing to do in polyamory is to speak honestly with each other.

About monogamy. Men often like to say: "Well, we are polygamous by nature and it is natural for us to have a harem." It has already been noted in previous chapters that this is not true. There are definitions imposed by society, state, and religion. Sure, truly monogamous people exist! There are those who fall in love once and for life, they love only one partner, and it's enough for them, and they don't pay attention to anyone else. In such relationships, the most important thing is honesty and understanding. Everything that is important is similar in monogamous and polyamorous relationships. All the core rules of polyamory are absolutely suitable for monogamy. If the monogamous marriage is honest, with setting agreements and boundaries, the partners will be open to each other and everything will be perfect.

If you can answer the following questions in the affirmative, then most likely you will prevail over jealousy. In the opposite case - it's better not to risk your feelings and avoid experiments with polyamorous relationships.

1. A person experiences deep feelings or passion for several people at the same time and wants to freely express these feelings.

2. A person allows relationships to develop naturally, without trying to squeeze them into frameworks too strict.

3. Having multiple partners is as normal for a person as close friendship with several people.

4. A person seeks to experience different types of romantic and sexual relationships and understands that one partner cannot satisfy all his or her desires.

5. A person wants to expand the existing relationship but does not want to deceive his/her partner and thus is ready to provide the same freedom for the said partner.

Chapter 8
Forms of Agreements Between Partners: Absolute Trust and Communication

Description of a healthy polyamorous relationship usually starts with mutual respect and openness between the participants. At the same time, partners can set certain boundaries and enter into agreements. Violation of these boundaries and agreements will harm their relations all the same as deception disrupts a monogamous union.

What are possible forms of polyamorous relationships?

1. **V** - this Latin letter denotes a situation when one person meets two others who are not connected by any relationship. By analogy with V, the forms N and W can exist - the shape of the letters hint at the number of partners, although the interpretations sometimes differ.

2. **Triangle** - three people who are in relationships with each other.

3. **Square** - four people in a relationship. Often, but not necessarily, two separate pairs enter a "square".

4. **Group** - more than four partners in a relationships with each other.

5. **Open marriages or relationships** - a couple, where both participants independently from each other meet with other people.

6. **Solo** - a person who meets with several people but does not distinguish a leading relationship and does not seek to live with one or all of his partners.

7. **Hierarchical polyamory** is the opposite of the previous situation: a person identifies "primary" relationships (they can be characterized by a high level of proximity, cohabitation, shared budget) and

"secondary". Moreover, the "secondary" partner is not necessarily less important but takes up less space in the everyday life of another.

Of course, all classifications are conditional: people themselves establish the rules and format of their relationship. The main thing is that the format and rules are discussed among all participants involved. Until you discuss with your partner exactly what kind of relationship you are in, you cannot be completely sure of them.

You need to understand that from purely technical point of view, polyamory is most definitely not the best solution for everyone. The system of three people, where everyone has their own schedule, their own interests, and their own plans for the future, is much more difficult to consider than a system of two. Therefore, it is critical that the fundamental principles are respected by everyone. This simplifies the task.

The basic principle: all participants understand and agree, in fact, and not just in words, that they are not the only ones that share resources:

- Resources are different things: time, attention, love, libido, mutual assistance, material things

- How exactly the resources are divided is subject to personal agreements between partners within a polyamorous relationship.

To better understand the complexity, it seems to me that a good analogy with multitasking on the phone will do. The early iPhone models were frankly single-tasked. Exiting one application meant that this application could not at all remind of itself. It does not receive processor time, access to the speaker, microphone, camera and the Internet, etc. The only exceptions were system applications like calendars and alarms. Now background applications are already supported (there are push notifications, there is background app refresh, or applications like Skype, with a running call that continue to work when you exit them). But it's still very limited support, and screen-sharing for true multitasking has not yet been done.

Engineers will understand deeply the range of tasks that need to be solved so that multitasking could be possible. There are many more difficulties:

1. **Sharing resources**. How to make sure that less interesting applications do not consume too much? (The active application is interesting by default, the user has clearly chosen it, but what to do with the background ones?). Especially, it concerns the battery consumption, but not only it: also the consumption of processor time (and the heat generated

2. **Privacy, security**. How to take care of sharing access so that one application does not "peep" at what another is doing? But at the same time, how to avoid implementing too much restrictions so that information exchange between applications was still possible.

3. **Management of notifications**. How to allow a background application to interrupt the active one in order to inform something, but at the same time prevent abuse and give the user good control as to which interrupts are acceptable and which are not?

These are complex tasks and, when negotiating a relationship in this way, sometimes you can feel like a phone on which you are trying to implement multitasking.

As you already understood, free relations have only one rule – honesty. All other conditions, norms and taboos are negotiated by partners in their own way. Therefore, uniform rules for all situations are downright impossible. In order to formulate everything succinctly and clearly, you need to spend time and meticulously discuss all the subtleties.

For example, you can rely on the following questions when you make your own rules for free love:

• How many sexual contacts can you have with one person?

• Is it possible to be friends or keep in touch with this person after sex?

• Is it possible to bring a temporary lover to the common house?

• Is it possible to introduce a temporary partner to a permanent one?

• What to do with those who want to continue the relationship, who want to make them serious?

These are just some examples. Also, be sure to discuss the rules of protection and agree to be honest in everything - no secrets.

But it also could happen like it happened with the heroes of the following story:

Olivia, 27

I'm 2.5 years older than Daniel. We first met when he just graduated from college. After that, for six years, I met him twice at parties. He managed to study in London, work in Nigeria, and then returned to the United States. Once Daniel called me, we went on a date and got married two weeks later. It was immediately clear that we had no reason to part.

We came to the format of open relationships right away. At that moment, I was in a romantic relationship with a woman, we lived with her. To be honest, I was acting wrong towards her because she knew that some Dany had appeared, but I got married without even telling her. Now, however, she is friends with him, we are all on good terms.

Initially, we agreed on how we see relationships with partners. We have created a bunch of rules. For example, warn in advance about upcoming sex with other people. But then it turned out that someone had a date, but he forgot to warn about it, and we changed the rules: we began to speak in fact. Then someone was on a business trip and forgot to talk about some kind of partner. It became obvious that the rules did not work, in the end we completely dropped them.

So, once again, you can choose whether to live with rules or without them. You just need to know yourself. And if it's difficult, in the last chapter, we will offer you a test to pass, and this test will help you understand your readiness for non-monogamy. Now let's look at another vital aspect of such a relationship - HEALTH. Any rules in a relationship can be created or broken, except for one - safe sex!

Chapter 9
Sexual Health:
Protected Sex and Periodic Testing

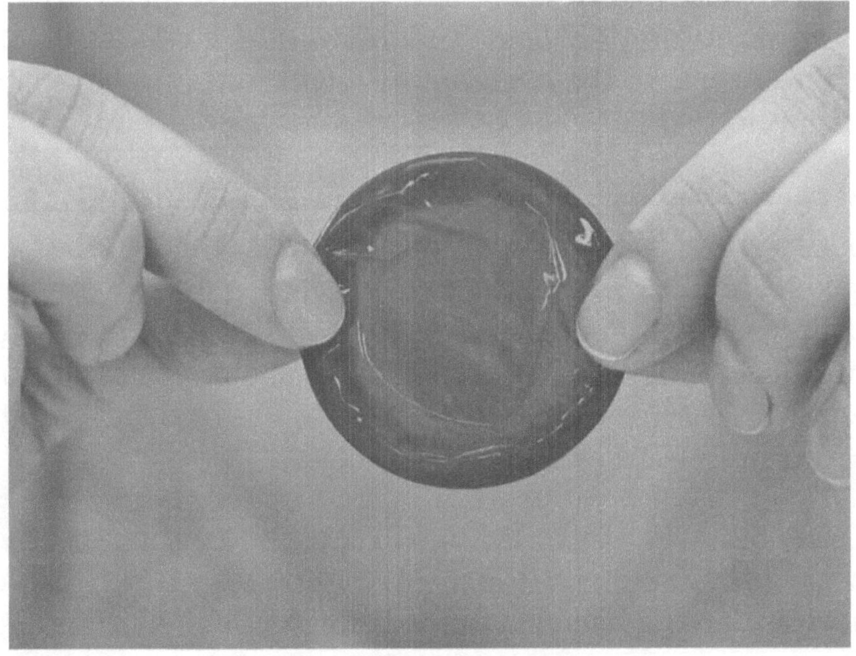

Sexual energy in polygamous relationships is very strong, and at the time of passion, it is likely to lose control of yourself and forget to use the means for safe sex. Moreover, if you have so many partners at the same time, even the most reliable contraceptives can fail.

Sexually transmitted diseases and infections (STDs) and unwanted pregnancy are serious reasons to pay special attention to safety during sex. The more sexual partners, the higher the risk of infection.

Although oral sex is considered safer than traditional sexual contact, it still has a health risk. Indeed, it implies close physical contact. You just need to be careful, no matter what, to whom, and how you do it. Therefore, take the necessary precautions and have sex with pleasure.

An active sex life helps us maintain good health, but, oddly enough, in polygamous families, the number of sexual acts does not increase. Like in monogamous couples, it can decrease over time. For example, due to physical fatigue, frequent stresses, in the face of emotional stress, and concurrently with deviations in reproductive system health.

Gynecologists and urologists attribute this to the microflora incompatibility. Men and women each have accompanying bacteria that reside inside their genitals. These bacteria might be either useful or harmful, depending on many conditions. The more sexual partners one has, the higher is the risk of awakening "sleeping" genital infections. As a result, usual practice is to have a course of treatment, including even those who are probably healthy and have no apparent signs of infection.

With modern, polygamous relationships, it is imperative that you take tests to make sure you are not carrying any STDs before having unprotected sex. This is necessary insofar as many sexually transmitted diseases may have subtle symptoms or no symptoms at all (so called asymptomatic carrier state).

In addition, if the couple does not plan to add to a family, then, without the use of condoms, it is worth using contraception: birth control pills, an intrauterine device, etc. However, no such remedy can guarantee complete protection against unwanted pregnancy.

Gynecologists warn: increase in number of male sexual partners for a woman means increase in the risk of developing endocrine disorders. They are manifested by menstrual cycle disorders or inflammation of the pelvic organs. According to statistical data, in most cases men are carriers of pathogens responsible for these disorders. The female body is more susceptible to infections.

Given this increased risk, it would be prudent to use such forms of protection - condoms, cofferdams, and medical gloves can prevent contact with body fluids (such as blood, vaginal fluid, semen, rectal mucus) and other biological and non-biological surfaces (such as skin, hair, and general objects) during sexual activity.

• **External condoms** can be used to cover the penis, hands, fingers, or other parts of the body during sexual penetration or stimulation. They are most often made from latex, and can also be made from synthetic materials, including polyurethane and polyisoprene.

• **Cofferdam** (originally used in dentistry) is a latex sheet used to protect against STD transmission during oral sex. It is usually used as a barrier between the mouth and vulva during cunnilingus or between the mouth and anus during anilinction.

• **Inner condoms** (also called female condoms) are inserted into the vagina or anus before sexual intercourse. These condoms are made of polyurethane or nitrile. If external and internal condoms are used at the same time, they may break due to friction between materials during sexual activity.

• **Medical gloves** made from latex, vinyl, nitrile, or polyurethane can be used as home-made cofferdams during oral sex or can cover hands, fingers, or other parts of the body during penetration or sexual stimulation, such as masturbation.

Condoms, cofferdams and gloves can also be used to cover sex toys, such as dildos, during sexual intercourse, stimulation, or penetration. If a sex toy should be used in more than one place or for more than one partner, you can use a condom, rubber dam, or glove to cover it and then change covering when changing places of use. Oil-based grease can deteriorate the structure of latex condoms, rubber dam or gloves, reducing their effectiveness in protecting against STDs.

There is a risk that a high tide of passion can make lovers forget about safety and proceed to sex without protection. Therefore, any step in a mono- or polygamous relationship requires awareness and responsibility.

Previous studies have shown that gay and bisexual men who are in a constant relationship are much more likely to practice unprotected anal sex with their main partners than single men with random partners.

Anal sex

Protected anal penetration is considered high-risk sexual activity, as the thin tissues of the anus and rectum can be easily damaged. Even slight injuries can lead to bacterial and viral infections, including HIV. Anal sex includes penetration into the anus with fingers, hands, or sex toys such as dildos. In addition, condoms are more likely to burst during anal sex than during vaginal sex, which increases the risk of STD transmission.

The main risk that people experience when doing anal sex is HIV transmission. Other possible infections include hepatitis A, B, and C, intestinal parasitic infections, such as Giardia, and bacterial infections, such as E. coli.

It is important that a man washes and cleans his penis after anal sex if he intends to penetrate the vagina. Bacteria from the rectum are easily transferred to the vagina, which can cause infections of the vagina and urinary tract.

To make anal sex safer, participants must ensure that the anal area is clean, and the rectum is empty. A partner who experiences anal penetration should be able to relax. Regardless of whether there is anal penetration with a finger or penis, a condom is the best barrier method to prevent transmission of STDs. Enemas should not be used because they can increase the risk of HIV infection, venereal lymphogranuloma, and proctitis.

HIV

For many people, positive HIV status is an inviolable taboo for having sex. Most people perceive a possible HIV infection as the end of their sexual life; in turn, most HIV-negative people do not consider any kind of physical intimacy with an infected partner.

At the same time, people living with HIV are people living a full, long life with a chronic, but manageable disease. They desire and deserve love and intimacy, like everyone else, and the relationship itself can serve as their best motivation for therapy.

Of course, it is possible that a person chooses a partner with the same HIV status. However, "mixed unions" are also very common: in the USA there are at least 140,000 serodiscordant couples. In countries where HIV is especially prevalent, more than 3% of all couples are serodiscordant, and two-thirds of HIV-positive people are in such relationships. [25]

For such couples, there is no single strategy regarding intimacy. Sometimes partners agree only on emotional closeness, or perhaps have a polygamous relationship while having sex with other partners. Some choose sex without penetration, or always use condoms. Sex with an HIV-positive partner who has an undetectable viral load is considered safer than sex with a person who is not confident in their status.

Vasilios Papapitsios:

I became HIV positive when I was 19 years old. Now I am 28 and only now have I begun to speak openly about my status. I lived in North Carolina, a very intolerant state that approved the HIV prevention program for drug users only in 2019. Then, due to the existing stigma, it was much easier for me to imagine relationships or just casual sex exclusively with HIV-positive partners.

Elijah McKinnon:

I'm from San Francisco. I grew up in a fairly liberal family, in which they spoke freely about sex and various sexually transmitted diseases, including HIV. My parents are in an open relationship, and some of my relatives died from AIDS. I have many HIV-positive friends and they are still alive. It was a surprise for me that some people try not to talk about their status. I knew that I had to control my own status and understand how best to protect myself. I mean not only STDs, but also mental and emotional health.

Sex toys

Putting a condom on a sex toy provides better sexual hygiene and can help prevent transmission of disease or infection. If the sex toy is shared, the condom must be replaced when the toy is used by another partner. Some sex toys are made of porous materials. Pores could trap viruses and bacteria, which makes thorough cleaning of sex toys necessary. It is preferable to do this using cleaning products specifically designed for sex toys. The glass is not porous, and medical glass sex toys are more easily sterilized between applications.

All sex toys must be properly cleaned and disinfected after use. The way you clean a sex toy depends on the type of material it is made of. Some sex toys can be boiled. Most sex toys are provided along with tips on how to better clean and store them. These instructions should be carefully followed. A sex toy should be cleaned not only when other people use it, when it is used in different parts of the body (for example, in the mouth, vagina or anus).

The sex toy should be checked regularly for scratches or tears that can become a dwelling place for bacteria. It is best if the damaged sex toy is replaced with a new undamaged one. Pregnant women should use even more strict hygienic measures when using sex toys. Sharing any type of sex toy that can have blood on it, such as whips or needles, is not recommended and unsafe.

In conclusion, in polygamous relationships, you can minimize the risk if you follow these tips.

First of all, in order to enjoy safe oral, vaginal and anal sex, all participants need to have enough male and female condoms, as well as rubberdams. Each time you change a partner or orifice, take off your protection and put on a new one. If you use sex toys such as anal balls, vibrators or dildos, take those made of non-porous material (glass or silicone) and do not use them on more than one person without cleaning the surfaces. For easier use, wear condoms on toys to minimize risk.

Participants can also simply observe each other or limit the interaction during which two or more people move close to each other, but, in fact, you are not touching anyone but your main partner. Things like passionate kisses, petting, touching the genitals, solo or mutual masturbation and the use of sex toys pose very little risk. If you really trust your partners, you can experiment with them, playing erotic and role-playing games, doing fetishism, doing erotic photo sessions or even practicing various types of BDSM (Bondage & Discipline, Domination & Submission). Even with the highest level of responsibility for your health and the health of partners, it is necessary to periodically undergo comprehensive tests which confirm the health of the genitourinary system, as well as the whole body. This will ensure the quality of life and bring satisfaction to each participant in the relationship.

Chapter 10

The Level of Personal Growth and Responsibility in Polyamorous Relationships

In the previous chapters, you probably recognized yourself in places, or caught yourself thinking that polyamory always belonged to another type of person.

However, by virtue of circumstances, you did not dare to enter into "unconventional relations," fearing the rejection of society.

If you want, you can gain the experience of any relationship and consider it just an adventure in your biography. Then you will not worry - how society looks at it, whether you are protected, hoping for the support of the law, whether you have any rights and whether you can claim recognition of these rights by everyone. With such a vision, you can do anything without breaking the law and harming others. Responsibility lies with you only.

Only a mature person is able to evaluate and directly name (even for himself) his true desires and aspirations.

1. If non-monogamy is your belief/attitude and you are aware of this.

2. If you understand how it will affect all areas of your life, and at the same time remain true to yourself - it means that you are a mature person, and no one has the right to interfere with your choice.

Who is this mature person?

Psychological maturity is a special state of mental processes and worldview that allows a person to self-actualize.

There are 4 components of such a person:

- responsibility;

- tolerance;

- self-improvement;

- positive thinking, positive attitude towards the world.

What will a non-monogamous relationship bring?

Pleasant discoveries, respect for oneself and partners, happiness and satisfaction with relationships or ...An extreme and traumatizing adventure for the psyche, due to unpreparedness and ignorance of risks that lie along this path? Everything depends on individual maturity!

Polyamory and open relations require great concentration, awareness and self-understanding. It's much easier to hurt yourself or your partner than in traditional family relationships, which are governed by clear patterns. There are no binding rules in an open union, and each decision is made anew under new conditions.

How to determine your maturity?

Interestingly, a mature personality, according to Maslow has the following characteristics [26]:

- Ability to accept oneself and others as they are.

- Lack of predatory, artificial forms of behavior and rejection of such behavior by other people.
- Adequate perception of reality, free from the influence of stereotypes, needs and prejudices.
- Interest in the unknown.
- Business focus. This means that such a person is less occupied with himself and more with his life mission.
- Spontaneity of manifestations, simplicity and naturalness. Such a person observes traditions, rituals and ceremonies, but at the same time treats them with a proper sense of humor. This is the correct conformism, not automatic.
- Independence from the environment.
- The position of detachment in relation to many phenomena. This allows them to give in less to external influences.
- Stability under the influence of stress factors.
- Unhazed perception, curiosity: the ability to find something new in things and phenomena already known.
- Friendship with other mature personalities: a narrow circle of people with whom relations are quite deep.
- A sense of community with humanity as a whole.

- Steady internal moral standards. Such people have a keen sense of justice, keenly feel good and evil.
- Willingness to learn from others.
- Perception of life with a good sense of humor.
- Critical attitude to the culture to which they belong.
- Creativity in all matters.

Polyamoria implies acceptance of one´s partners' independence, rejection of any possessive attitude towards the partner(s), and respect for their personal boundaries. A conscious and voluntary rejection of any imaginable rights of ownership of another person is, as you know, the best vaccine against jealousy, fears, love madness and emotional dependence.

Weigh your spiritual strength

Do you have enough in you to experience full-scale love fo several people at once and respect their needs at the same time? Most people in relationships, like in business, always want to get more than they give. But love doesn't work like that, and in polyamory, in the "multi-lover-ness" – this statement is even truer. To get a lot from such relationship, you will have to give even more generously: listen to all your partners, support them, take care, and for this you need to have great supply of physical, mental and emotional resources at the first place.

Great pleasure and great work — this is the duality of the beautiful phenomenon of polyamory.

Chapter 11

This test will help you determine your readiness for a polyamorous relationship.

Just choose the answer that best suits your character and calculate the amount of points.

At the end of the test, find your result

Test

Could you be in a non-monogamous relationship?

1. What do you think of non-monogamous relationships?

- It is a great way to preserve the novelty and brightness in a relationship 1

- I would like to try to be in such a relationship 2

- I wouldn't like to try and don't understand how people can endure it 3

2. Can you be called a jealous person?

- No, I do not know this feeling 1

- It depends on situation 2

- Yes, I have certain problems with jealousy. 3

3. Are you true to your soulmate?

- Yes, but I think that a little freedom will not hurt. 2

- Yes, and I don't understand how you can live differently 3

- Not. I do not remain faithful to my partner. 1

4. Do you want to get married and start a family?

- Yes 3

- No 2

- I don't know yet 1

5. Who are you closer with?

- With parents 3

- With friends 2

- What do you mean, closer? 1

6. What quality should your partner have?

- Honesty 2

- Sense of humor 1

- Kindness 3

7. How would you like to spend a Saturday night?

- Sit at the bar with friends 1

- Lie down at home and watch a movie 3

- Walk with someone 2

8. What kind of movie would you choose to watch with your partner?

- Comedy 2

- Thriller 1

- Melodrama 3

Results:

8-16

1. Perhaps by free relations you mean different things. And not radical changes in personal life. Or maybe not. Who knows...?

In any case, in an open relationship, you could bloom again.

You are not one of those who are jealous of your partner. And you want the same in your address.

In addition, you have long revised the concept of traditional relations and came to the conclusion that a person should have much more freedom of action.

17-24

2. This kind of relationship makes you uncomfortable. Even the mere thought that someone else might be next to your soulmate is an unpleasant sensation. You would not be able to hold out for a month in an open relationship. After all, for you only one loved one is enough for happiness. You greatly appreciate the traditional understanding of the family and cannot change these principles.

Chapter 12
Conclusion

So, you have learned that monogamy is not the only form of relationship on our planet. Single, polygamy, marriage types such as White (spiritual) marriage, Lavender marriage, Interfaith marriage, Organized marriage, Original (creative) marriage, Open marriage, Polyamory, Polyandry, Polygyny, Parent marriage, Initial (trial) marriage, Partnership. There are also forms of open sexual relations: threesome, swinging.

You have learned that in the history of mankind all these forms have existed for centuries in different countries of our multicultural planet.

Attitude towards non-monogamy has changed in society from complete rejection to legal existence. Literature, art and cinema have created wonderful works about this phenomenon. Non-monogamy has given to psychologists an enormous amount of material for research. People develop new approaches to such phenomena as infidelity and jealousy. Once again we remembered that with the most conservative and with the most liberal forms of relations - the most important thing is to maintain physical and mental health. And what is surprising - each form of marriage or relationship is definitely a launching pad for self-improvement and personal growth. Kaleidoscope of Polyamory is a fascinating and very interesting tool for the soul and the body. Are you ready to master this tool or just look into it with curiosity? We hope this book has helped you to find an answer that suits your needs perfectly.

References

1. "Polyamorous relationships may be the future of love." *Melissa Hogenboom*
2. Wikipedia
3. "The end of romance: what will replace marriage and monogamy?" *Daria Shipacheva*, Forbes Contributor
4. "Non-love is a disease." Text: *Susanna Alperina, Tatyana Khoroshilova*
5. Quote from the book: "Three comrades." *Erich Maria Remarque*
6. "Women's Polygamia: A New Trend or Tragedy". *Grechanovsky, Viktor*. Doctor, candidate of medical sciences, psychotherapist.
7. Site. *Allah Knowing*
8. "Scientists rated the level of happiness in polygamous relationships." Journal of Social and Personal Relationships.
9. "Roxy." Women's magazine
10. "Marriages between man and robot can be legalized in 2050." *Alexandra Samuilkina*
11. "Open marriage." Wikipedia
12. "The paradox of polygamy I: Why most Americans are polygamous." Satoshi Kanazawa
13. "Polygamy". Wikipedia
14. "Strengthening polyamory in the modern world." tjournal.ru
15. "Polyamorous marriages - next in line for legalization?" Melissa Hogenboom
16. "Fall in love with a married couple. Why polyamory is called the future of relations." *Stadnik Stadnik*

17. "Irina Khakamada said that she and her husband have free relations." Passion.Ru., women's magazine

18. "Open relations - to be together, but to remain free." *Ekaterina Gudkova*

19. "Strengthening polyamory in the modern world." tjcache.pw

20. "Love stories of famous people." blog.i.ua

21. "100 great lovers." *Muromov Igor*

22. "Charlie Chaplin: 10 facts from the life of the great actor." afisha.nyc

23. "Relationship characteristics and motivations behind agreements among gay male couples: differences by agreement type and couple serostatus." US National Library of Medicine National Institutes of Health

24. "Pros and cons: how couples with different HIV statuses have sex." Safe.step.

25. "15 signs of psychological maturity by Abraham Maslow." fit4brain.com